ATYPICAL

Best Wishes

June 2025

ATYPICAL

FIVE STRATEGY RULES FOR A NEW WORLD

PRATEEK RAJ

Published by Westland Business, an imprint of Westland Books, a division of Nasadiya Technologies Private Limited, in 2025

No. 269/2B, First Floor, 'Irai Arul', Vimalraj Street, Nethaji Nagar, Alapakkam Main Road, Maduravoyal, Chennai 600095

ISBN: 9789360454531

10 9 8 7 6 5 4 3 2 1

The views and opinions expressed in this work are the author's own and the facts are as reported by him, and the publisher is in no way liable for the same.

Typeset by Mukul

Printed at Thomson Press (India) Ltd

‘I tell my students, “When you get these jobs that you have been so brilliantly trained for, just remember that your real job is that if you are free, you need to free somebody else. If you have some power, then your job is to empower somebody else. This is not just a grab-bag candy game.”’

—Toni Morrison

Dedicated to my wonderful colleague and mentor, late Professor Ganesh Prabhu, who gave the name 'Strategic Stewardship' to my MBA course, which is the basis for this book.

Contents

Introduction xi

Rule 0

VALUE ~~INTELLECT~~ EMPATHY

I. Learning from the Fringes 2
II. Intelligence in the Age of AI 10
III. Strategic Design Thinking 15

Rule 1

LEAD FROM THE ~~TOP~~ GROUND

1. Strategy 101: Inimitable Capabilities 24
2. Capabilities Lie in Relationships 30
3. Nurturing Trust in Organisations 36
4. From the Ground to the C-Suite 44
5. Leading with a Himalayan Mindset 50

Rule 2

PURSUE ~~PROFIT~~ INNOVATION

6. Dirty Strategies 62
7. Self-correcting Markets 73
8. The Role of Regulators 80

9. Good Strategies Innovate 89
10. Know Your Village for Creative Destruction 98

Rule 3
HEAR THE ~~TYPICALS~~ ATYPICALS

11. Design Isn't Neutral 108
12. Products Have Externalities 113
13. Atypical Stakeholders Know First 125
14. Moral and Amoral Drift 134
15. Embracing Atypical Testing 141

Rule 4
~~WIN~~ NURTURE

16. Public Goods Capitalism 154
17. The Future of Business 169
18. Philanthropy-owned Businesses 181
19. What Good Can Businesses Do? 191
20. Bring the Community Together with a Vision 201

Conclusion 208
Notes 211
Index 222
Acknowledgements 237

Introduction

'It was the best of times, it was the worst of times.' English writer Charles Dickens wrote these words over a hundred and fifty years ago (1859) as he described late eighteenth-century England and France. We could use these words to describe our times as well—the early twenty-first century, an era of grand possibilities and cataclysmic challenges.

From work to family to food and fuel, life in the twenty-first century is rapidly transforming. What kind of century will this be? A century of progress, where everyone has enough to live well, or a century of environmental and economic decay, where few get a lot, and others are stripped even of their environment? Our times are especially unique and atypical in human history, as we are Generation One, which must confront the social and environmental consequences of our actions at a planetary scale, unlike any other generation in the past. Our future will be shaped by all of us and by the choices we make at work, at home and in our communities as leaders, builders and carers.

The Twenty-first Century: Atypical Times

The best of times ...

We live in a time when life and liveability on the planet itself are at a crossroads. India and China, giants with over a third of the global population, are surging ahead economically, lifting millions from poverty. The reach of technology, from mobile phones to the internet and now AI, has knit even the most isolated areas into a global village. Marginalised groups are finding platforms for visibility and representation like never before. For many, including women and queer people, there hasn't been an era better than this one.

... and the worst of times

However, this era is marred by increasing wealth disparity, conflicts, human displacement and environmental degradation. The gravest of these challenges is climate change, disproportionately affecting those who least contributed to it, such as the people in Sudan, Madagascar and South Asia. Our cities are heating up to over 50 degrees centigrade and will soon be unliveable, facing cascading issues like acute water scarcity and desertification.

The legacy of industrialisation, synonymous with GDP, income, consumption and economic growth, has also left a trail of waste and ecological harm. English writer H.G. Wells, commenting on this in 1918, said, 'At the advent of steam and electricity, the muse of history holds her nose and shuts her eyes.'[1] While environmentalism arose in response in the late nineteenth century, it has not been enough to stem the tide of ecological damage. In this context, the words of Indian leader Mahatma Gandhi become poignant, who in 1928 expressed, 'God forbid that India should ever take to industrialism after the manner of the West ... If an entire nation of 300 million took to similar economic exploitation, it would strip the world bare like locusts.'[2]

If you lead an organisation or hope to lead one someday, this book is for you. What kind of choices should you make to make this a better century? Should you be revolutionary or incremental? Set up entirely new economic systems? Invent new organisational forms? Or retool existing systems more purposefully? In this book, we delve into these questions. These questions are not abstract enquiries. They shape the world around us every day.

Our world today runs on rules and assumptions established in the past. But have they been scrutinised for suitability for our times and the future? We must scrutinise assumptions about intelligence (*Is having a high IQ a mark of intelligence?*), leadership (*Is leadership a position?*), purpose (*Is profit the bottom line?*), design (*Is design for the 'common man'?*) and legacy (*Is being the apex—the best—the ultimate goal?*) so that we can lead, build and nurture organisations based on a set of principles that are suitable for the challenges and opportunities of the world today.

If we follow the wrong rules, we will perpetuate the old toxic patterns, patterns that have turned our green cities into concrete jungles with a few 'exclusive' green communities as trophies, or those that turned our workplaces into toxic arenas where employees do backbreaking work only to serve a few who live grand, decadent lives. But if we correct the course, rethinking the frames with which we see the world and the rules with which we build it, a better world can emerge, a world that has a place for us all—*a world with dignity at its core*.

In this book, let us explore the rules of strategy and management that can create organisations, workplaces and societies that are truly inclusive—not just for us, but also for the planet. We need new rules of progress, where maximising the dignity of life and nature is the bottom line, not merely profit or GDP growth. Moreover, these rules must be practical. I do not intend to weave a grand vision for a new world like Karl Marx or Milton Friedman. Who shall implement those grand visions? Governments and business tycoons? Instead, my focus in this book is on our organisations and the people who build them—all of us in the various roles we play. Can adding some simple, arguably atypical, rules to follow at work and in life create better and more conscious organisations around us, which can then contribute to building a better world?

I present the following simple rules that, in my understanding, can create organisations best suited for building a sustainable and inclusive world:

- Rule 1: Lead from the ~~top~~ ground.
- Rule 2: Pursue ~~profit~~ innovation.
- Rule 3: Hear the ~~typicals~~ atypicals.
- Rule 4: ~~Win~~ Nurture.

I developed these rules while researching[3] and teaching Strategic Stewardship, a course I designed for management students at IIM Bangalore. This book is a result of my work at the Inclusive Markets Lab at IIMB and the long-term support of the Stigler Center at the University of Chicago Booth School of Business.

Underpinning these four rules is the fifth rule—or rule zero—laying the epistemological foundation: *value* ~~intellect~~ *empathy*. I begin with this rule now.

Rule 0

VALUE ~~INTELLECT~~ EMPATHY

'Too much energy in your country is spent developing the mind instead of the heart.'[1]

—The Dalai Lama

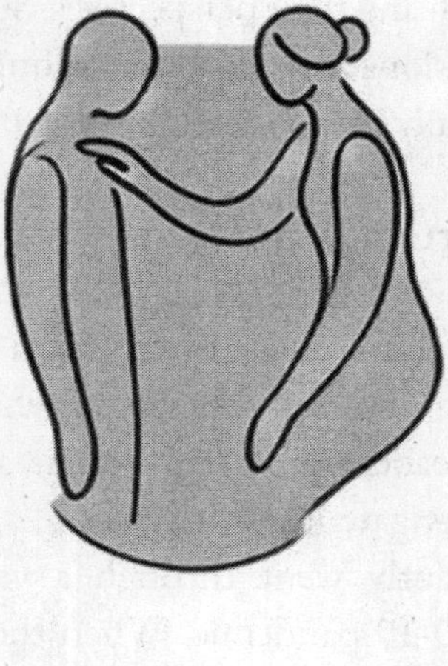

I. Learning from the Fringes

We are always learning. Learning does not come just from reading books, analysing data, working on a project or making field visits. It also comes from standing in the shoes of others, especially those who are unlike us—atypical—and understanding them and their perspectives. Such empathy can help us make better decisions and take others along, and is a critical tool for learning, especially in an uncertain world.

Leading an Uncertain World

The world is never static, and we must learn about it as it evolves. This is even more important for those who lead organisations, as the value of a leader comes from their ability to understand uncertainty and navigate it effectively.

The world recently went through a very uncertain period during the COVID-19 pandemic. When the number of affected patients began to grow exponentially in late December 2019 and early January 2020 in Wuhan, China, the local official response to these mysterious pneumonia-like cases was marked by a reluctance to disclose information to the rest of the country and consequently the world. Healthcare workers, including doctors, who wished to communicate their concerns about this new virus feared pushback if they shared their findings.

A local doctor, Li Wenliang, tried to warn the public about the novel coronavirus in late December 2020. But he was reprimanded and punished for 'spreading rumours'. In a tragic turn of events, Dr Li himself later contracted the disease while treating patients and died in February 2020, by which time information about the disease had been made public, leading to widespread grief in China and a rare government apology to his family.

The Chinese government's tight information and media control meant critical early warnings were ignored or not broadly disseminated. A team led by Hong Kong-based virologist Dr Guan Yi visited Wuhan on 21 January but, dismayed by the lack of transparency, commented that 'epidemiology experts and scientists do not seem to be welcomed in the city'.[2]

This opacity had two major consequences. First, it delayed a coordinated, informed response to the virus in China. If the early warnings of healthcare professionals had been disseminated transparently, measures like widespread testing, contact tracing and public awareness might have contained the virus more effectively in the epicentre.

Second, a faster global pandemic response was impaired. International health authorities and governments relied on official Chinese reports to understand the virus, including its transmissibility. On 14 January, the World Health Organization incorrectly stated, based on local reports, that there was 'no clear evidence of human-to-human transmission of the novel coronavirus (2019-nCoV) identified in Wuhan, China'.[3] The eventual acknowledgement of human-to-human transmission came only on 20 January 2020, which meant critical weeks were lost in pandemic preparation, delaying other countries' travel restrictions and health system preparations.

China imposed travel restrictions to and from Wuhan only on 23 January. If China had a system willing to listen to Wuhan's frontline doctors and health workers, the COVID-19 pandemic could have been contained earlier, potentially saving millions of lives.

Another older case in which listening to those at the periphery could have helped millions, arguably billions, was the case of poisoning by the American chemical giant DuPont. Since 1948, DuPont has manufactured Teflon, a chemical used to make cooking appliances and other surfaces non-sticky, in a Washington, West Virginia factory. Teflon was highly popular, earning DuPont a total income of nearly $1.1 billion over time.[4] However, the product contained C8 (perfluorooctanoic acid or PFOA). Over three decades (1980s–2010s), the toxicity of this chemical gradually came under intense public scrutiny. DuPont eventually phased out using C8 in Teflon production in 2015.

The dangers of C8 were not initially highlighted by DuPont's top management, government bureaucrats or employees. Instead, awareness emerged from the fringes—suppliers, workers, local fauna and the community. Information on C8's toxicity has been available since the 1960s from lab studies. DuPont executives became aware of the risks of the chemical to pregnant employees at least by 1981, following the discovery by its supplier 3M about deformities in rat foetuses exposed to C8. Two of the seven pregnant women working at the plant with direct C8 exposure also had children born with abnormalities.

In the mid-1990s, the Tennants, a farming family living near the factory's landfill, noticed deformities in their cattle and local fauna. When their cattle began dying from drinking water contaminated with C8, they filed a federal lawsuit against DuPont in 1999. This lawsuit, led by lawyer Robert Bilott, began a long-lasting discovery battle, exposing the extent of the damage caused by C8 and DuPont's cover-up. A subsequent class action lawsuit in 2001 filed by locals exposed to contaminated water led to the formation of a scientific panel in 2004. In 2012, this panel linked C8 to at least six diseases, affecting over 3,500 of the 70,000 impacted individuals exposed to the contaminated water. It is expected that C8 is present in the bloodstream of nearly all humans due to its widespread use. Without advocates like Robert Bilott, who united disparate stakeholders affected by C8, the world might still be unaware of Teflon's toxic effects.

The Limitations of Data

What do the above cases of COVID-19 and Teflon poisoning tell us? Including diverse atypical voices is not just a moral imperative but essential for health and social resilience. Those at the system's fringes often suffer first, and their voices are usually crucial for developing understanding.

Why are some voices not included, but others get a seat at the table? Power plays a critical role. A small farming family like the Tennants is nothing more than a nuisance for a corporation like DuPont, which is focused on maximising profit. For a local politician or health administrator of Wuhan trying to rise through the ranks, critical voices from the bottom saying something very troubling about a new disease are highly unsettling.

Those who lead organisations often love to hear how good their work is. Good feedback feels psychologically safe, and we get addicted to it. Imagine the lengths to which politicians and businesses go to quell bad news. They may tolerate powerful critical stakeholders, as they can do nothing about them. Still, it takes a genuine sense of citizenship and responsibility to include and engage with the critical voices of the powerless when they have an option not to.

What would you do if you were in their shoes? We cannot learn about the world, which is ever-changing, waiting for 'big' data.

Until the 2010s, DuPont claimed that the adverse effects of Teflon were overblown. It took an unprecedented large sample study of 70,000 people exposed to Teflon-contaminated water to establish its ill-health effects with statistical certainty. And this study came at a cost: time.

Some of its rare effects, like congenital disabilities, are yet to be established to date, as a large enough sample could not be constructed to observe pregnant women exposed to the toxin. However, if two of seven pregnant women who worked in the Teflon factory gave birth to children with birth defects, our human mind can infer with obvious confidence that this must have something to do with the chemical. But how would we run a study that establishes this link with statistical accuracy? Should we wait for action until the day there is enough data to say with certainty that Teflon causes congenital disabilities? Who would volunteer for such a study? Should we wait for enough congenital disabilities to occur before we can act? Should we have to wait for a few more industrial disasters—like the DuPont Teflon poisoning, the 1984 Bhopal Gas disaster, or the 1986 Chernobyl nuclear disaster—before we can say that, indeed, we need strict environmental and safety standards?

Additionally, the data collection process is deeply political and fraught with influences of power. Today, the world reels with the effects of climate change, yet a large population—an estimated 49 million in the United States alone—is still sceptical of it. This scepticism is often fuelled by international organisations invested in fossil fuels, which support 'climate denialism' and fund politicians, regulators and even academics who popularise such scepticism.[5] Similarly, DuPont has been alleged to have supported regulators and scientists who promoted scepticism towards the toxicity of Teflon. Wuhan administrators, too, tried to stall international scientists from studying their health system.[6]

Access to data also has biases. We also live in a world where social media platforms are often accused of spreading hate and promoting internet addiction. Do we have enough data to say conclusively that social media fuels hate or promotes addiction? Not yet, because the data which can be used to conduct such studies is proprietary data held by the same organisations accused of creating this addiction, out of reach of independent researchers.

Data cannot tell us the truth if the underlying data generation process has systemic biases. If one relies on results derived from flawed data, one may become a data-fed fool, which is worse than being ignorant.

When human life and dignity are at stake, we cannot wait for irrefutable data to appear before we act. We must *be alert*, *investigate* and *act* when dealing with emergencies. Are we prepared for such alertness? Do we have the skills to listen, detect and respond to uncertain situations by being widely vigilant?

The Importance of Stories

Stories are everywhere, and we cannot escape them even if we try to. We are always telling a story, and even a dry statistical analysis ultimately produces a story. Stories can be powerful if they become our call to action in a way that statistics cannot. We can learn from statistics that average temperatures will rise by 2 °C within a few decades, but this statistic does not inspire emotion in us. Even extreme weather events in distant places do not invoke action. But when we experience first-hand the increasing pangs of thirst as water becomes less readily available, or we hear how someone was paralysed due to heatstroke while stuck in traffic in Delhi's summer heat, we feel climate change in our bones.

We need to feel issues in our bones through direct experience or an evocative narration of someone else's story before we get called to action. This is why the best leaders are often those who can tell the best stories. However, while a lot gets said about the skill of telling stories, less is said about the skill of listening to them.

Listening to stories is essential for having a purpose in our actions. It is a well-known statistic that six million Jews were murdered during the Holocaust by the Nazis. But this information, although horrific in its own merit, still fails to describe the sheer evil of those actions. It is in this context that personal accounts of the Holocaust, like the 1960 memoir *Night* by Elie Wiesel, become the bedrock literature of human history, as they vividly paint the horrors of the Holocaust through the eyes of a survivor. It is not easy to remain unaffected and unshaken once one has read *Night*.

An excerpt from *Night*

On reaching the Auschwitz concentration camp,

> An SS came toward us wielding a club. He commanded: 'Men to the left! Women to the right!' Eight words spoken quietly, indifferently, without emotion. Eight simple, short words. Yet that was the moment when I left my mother. There was no time to think, and I already felt my father's hand press against mine: we were alone. In a fraction of a second, I could see my mother, my sister, move to the right. Tzipora was holding Mother's hand. I saw them walking farther and farther away; Mother was stroking my sister's blond hair, as if to protect her. And I walked on with my father, with the men. I didn't know that this was the moment in time and the place where I was leaving my mother and Tzipora forever. I kept walking, my father holding my hand.[7]

Wiesel's mother (Sarah) and sister (Tzipora) were murdered not much later on arrival, and his father (Chlomo) died of dysentery and other indignities due to forced labour months later. Elie survived to tell the tale, going on to win the 1986 Nobel Peace Prize.

We need to change the way we look at literature. Good literature, fact or fiction, is not just art—it is wholesome information that gives us a glimpse into someone's experiences, giving us access to their stories and improving our ability to listen. For example, the acclaimed 1978 poem 'Still I Rise' by African American writer Maya Angelou encapsulates the experiences of millions who have faced stigma due to their background and history.

From 'Still I Rise' by Maya Angelou

You may write me down in history
With your bitter, twisted lies,
You may trod me in the very dirt
But still, like dust, I'll rise.

Did you want to see me broken?
Bowed head and lowered eyes?
Shoulders falling down like teardrops,
Weakened by my soulful cries?

You may shoot me with your words,
You may cut me with your eyes,
You may kill me with your hatefulness,
But still, like air, I'll rise.[8]

In our everyday lives, we are often selective about the stories that we wish to hear. This rational inattention keeps us from voluntarily entering situations we do not want to be a part of. However, leaders must be attentive and empathetic listeners. If there are voices at the fringes of society that speak of the daily indignities people face due to problems we directly contribute to, we have a duty to listen attentively and feel their struggles in our bones, too.

II. Intelligence in the Age of AI

WE value being quick and efficient. But in a world where an artificial intelligence (AI) model can crunch millions of data points in seconds, an aspect of slow, immersive understanding will be increasingly valuable—empathy.

AI will likely replace many of our 'thinking' jobs in the coming decades, such as analytics and summarisation. By not getting swayed by emotions, AI may also be able to make more unbiased and rational decisions, especially when executing routine processes, replacing many bureaucratic jobs.

The power of AI is fundamentally based on processing inputs codified in the form of words, numbers and symbols. Its massive processing power allows AI to simultaneously give processed outputs to billions of coded inputs. So, any human job that relies on processing codified inputs—be it text or numbers—is at risk of being replaced by AI in the next few decades.

However, human beings do not learn through words. We experience the world around us and life within ourselves rather non-discreetly. Much of this experience—for example, what the sweet taste of a Malda mango is like, or what it is like to be a victim of discrimination—cannot be fully transmitted through words.

Computers can be fed the transmitted descriptions, but the very nature of experience is such that we cannot communicate it in its entirety.

Humans, having experienced something in full, have the privilege of a more complete form of knowledge, which computers do not. Philosopher John Searle's 'Chinese Room' example illustrates this, arguing that computers are like a language translator that can perfectly translate a language like Chinese by processing symbols in one form to another, but it does not understand what these symbols mean in the way that humans do.[9]

In the twenty-first century, our understanding of intelligence is changing. Intelligence grounded in empathy, lived experience and, more importantly, unique experiences cannot be replaced by AI. Those who bring such lived and unique experiences to the table will always have great value to offer to the knowledge economy.

Empathy: The Ability to Immerse Oneself

Empathy is our ability to stand in someone else's shoes and see the world from their perspective without our judgements creeping in. It is easy to empathise with—or understand the perspective of—someone much like us. But it takes practice and time to listen to the stories of and empathise with those who are different from us.

We often caricature 'others' who are not like us and simplify their experiences into one-liners when we know intrinsically that our lives cannot be simplified the same way. Every time we make a racist, casteist, sexist, homophobic, transphobic or other such parochial remark about anyone or any community, we walk away from intelligence, as we paint a very shallow picture of someone's life. Not only is such snap and reductionist judgement immoral, but it is also profoundly unintelligent. It indicates a lack of empathy, as our understanding lacks insight and depth.

Living with empathy is a skill that allows us to have a higher-resolution understanding of someone else's life and their stories. Not having this skill means walking through life with a pixelated understanding of others.

There is some debate on whether empathy can be genuinely taught or if it is intrinsic to some people and not to others. Evidence suggests that empathy indeed can be taught. Many religions emphasise the importance of developing empathy, compassion and kindness through various practices, such as the Metta meditation in Buddhism. In the Metta meditation, the learner first develops understanding and compassion for oneself, then towards a friend, then towards a neutral acquaintance, then towards someone perceived as an enemy, and finally towards all four of these people at once. It is said that Gautama Buddha would do the Metta meditation first thing in the morning as he woke up, such was his belief in its effectiveness.

However, could the adoption of these practices be self-selection? That is, more empathetic people see the value in these practices more than others, and hence, they adopt them in their lives. If we went around teaching empathy-developing practices randomly to people, would it bear any fruit? Field experiments, such as Canada-based Roots of Empathy, suggest empathy can be learnt.[10]

An accredited programme for children below eight years of age, Roots of Empathy teaches empathy to children with 'babies as teachers'. In the programme, an infant and their parent visit local classrooms with a trained instructor multiple times for a year. The students observe the baby and its development, labelling the baby's feelings and intentions, and then reflect on their own. The programme has been tested in numerous randomised controlled trials across countries and cultural contexts, and the approach has been found to reduce aggression like bullying and increase cognitive (perspective-taking), emotional (sharing the feelings of others) and compassionate (prosocial behaviours like helping) empathy.

A practical way to integrate a seemingly 'soft' concept like empathy in our hard-nosed world of business and management is by developing the art of immersive listening. Immersive listening requires us to sit with someone or a group and give patient attention to their stories and emotions, suspending judgement and holding genuine conversations that allow us to immerse ourselves in their worlds.

Immersive listening can only work if it involves a suspension of presumptions and judgements that we make about ourselves and others. We are all judgemental, and often, these judgements are subconscious, i.e., implicit. A salient example of implicit bias is homophily, our liking for someone similar to us. These biases affect all of us and require awareness and attention to keep them from clouding our judgement.

Genuine conversations also require us to be watchful of power dynamics. For example, an employer holds inherent power over their employees, influencing how comfortable employees may feel in expressing themselves and opening up in a conversation under such asymmetric power dynamics. Authentic, immersive listening is possible only when an equal—secure and genuinely friendly—power dynamic is nurtured between the listener and the speaker.

The method of immersion in someone's world resembles the ethnographic approach. During the colonial period, European ethnographers would actively immerse themselves in the worlds of their colonial subjects to 'understand' their world better. However, the insights generated from such studies were coloured by prejudice, often perpetuating racism and expanding the colonial enterprise by portraying subjects as 'barbaric'. Today, creating hierarchies across cultures and 'races' is considered a pseudoscience, and we have developed appreciation for the wisdom of so-called 'primitive' societies. For example, we are learning from the water harvesting and soil conservation practices of forest-dwelling societies, and about multiple genders and 'twin' souls from the Native American people, realising that our ideas about society and progress are often socially constructed and constantly evolving based on who is in power.

Bias	Example Statement
Attribution bias	'She failed the project because she is lazy, but I failed because I had too much on my plate.'
Attractiveness bias	'He is good-looking, so he must be very good at managing himself.'
Blind spot bias	'I am very objective and unbiased, unlike most people.'
Dunning Kruger effect	'I have read a lot about Vietnam, so I know a lot about Southeast Asia.'
Halo bias	'She is a great speaker, so she must be a great employee.'
Homophily	'I like him because we both went to the same university.'
Horn bias	'He fumbled in his presentation, so he must be a lousy employee.'
Just world hypothesis	'If she is in trouble, this must be a result of her own actions.'
Naïve realism	'He thinks so differently from me. He is letting his subjectivity cloud his judgement.'
Outgroup bias	'Our team's ideas are always better than those of that other department.'
Status quo bias	'We've done things this way, so this is the valid way of doing things.'
Stereotyping	'He is gay (old), so he can't be good at sports (technology).'

III. Strategic Design Thinking

Now that we have discussed some epistemological concepts, let us combine these insights into a framework that can be used in daily work and organisational processes to solve problems or identify opportunities. At the core of our discussion is the design thinking approach—'a human-centred approach to innovation—anchored in understanding customers' needs, rapid prototyping, and generating creative ideas'.[11] Let us retool this approach to go beyond its general constituency of product design to handle truly complex problems holistically by involving multiple stakeholders. Let us call it the strategic design thinking process.[12]

The strategic design thinking process helps us develop a more granular picture of our world by uncovering the various codifiable and un-codifiable needs, wants, desires, issues and asks of multiple stakeholders. We can divide this process into a few steps.

1. List diverse stakeholders

The first and the most crucial step in the strategic design thinking process is listing the stakeholders. A limited list of stakeholders that ignores certain types can lead to vastly different conclusions. It can also render the very design thinking exercise less credible. Many stakeholders tend to be invisible or ignored; enough time must be given to consider a diverse set of stakeholders. Listing stakeholders is likely an ongoing and iterative process, as the design process will uncover new stakeholders that might not have been considered initially.

Stakeholders, Archetypes and Personas

Diversity exists within a stakeholder group. For example, a customer can be of various kinds and segmented by identity, personality, age, gender, income, etc. Identifying these different archetypes helps make a more detailed stakeholder engagement. The stakeholder archetype is the unit of stakeholder engagement for us; we call this unit a persona. There needs to be a balance here: personas should not be so broad that only generic, uninteresting statements can be made about them. Personas should also not be so narrow that collating their insights becomes an issue.

For example, when considering customers as a stakeholder, a young female MBA professional working in a metropolitan city can be an archetype. Her persona can be developed with design thinking, by standing in her shoes and identifying her needs and issues.

2. Stand in their shoes

The next stage involves actual stakeholder engagement. Both secondary research and immersive stakeholder engagement are needed to stand in a stakeholder's shoes. Secondary sources, such as demographic and economic data or newspaper and journal articles, help develop a preliminary understanding of a stakeholder, although such sources must be viewed with healthy scepticism and an open mind, as they too can have their own biases.

The core activity of the strategic design thinking process is immersive listening and actual stakeholder engagement.

Stakeholder conversations are never ten-minute surveys or interviews. They must include structured and unstructured questions—a few common/structured questions, for example, 'What motivated you to do this job/use this product/move to this place?', or 'How do you imagine your life five years from now?'. These can then lead to more organic follow-up conversations.

A sincere design thinker trying to develop an understanding of stakeholders may spend long hours to understand their lives. During the stakeholder engagement, the interviewees' emotions and body language should not be ignored, and it also helps to ask them how they will respond to different (real or hypothetical) scenarios. Once the stakeholder engagement is completed, the design thinker can develop interesting and insightful personas (think of them as archetypal characters in a script) for different stakeholder archetypes.

3. Identify their needs and issues

The personas help better identify the needs, wants, desires, issues and asks of various stakeholder archetypes. If personas are identified effectively, each stakeholder-archetype group will have unique needs, wants, desires, issues and asks.

A natural question may arise: Why must we divide a person's desires into many steps? What are needs, wants, desires, issues and asks? We do so because of implicit biases. We are often willing to listen only to the needs of some (for example, someone poor) and the desires of others.

Needs	Immediate requirements, which in someone's understanding are necessary for their sustenance and survival. E.g., a decent house, income, safety net, clean environment.

Wants	That which, in someone's understanding, will make their lives visibly better. E.g., a spacious house, stable income, group of reliable friends, garden at home.
Desires	That which will be good to have in life, but non-fulfilment will not affect the basics of life. E.g., large business, beach house, becoming an astronaut or CEO.
Issues	Recurring problems or concerns that bother someone. These could pertain to an organization or personal issues that need to be addressed.
Asks	Pointed demands a persona has from a system to improve their lives, fulfil needs and wants, resolve issues and bring dreams closer.

4. Identify proximate and ultimate factors

A stakeholder map containing the needs, wants, desires, issues and asks of various personas of a system gives us a snapshot of recurring themes and emerging patterns.[13] For example, while GDP seems to be the primary obsession for policymakers perched at the very top, if policymakers did a grounded design study, they would find that various stakeholders speak of issues like water and environment (air, trees, weather) that directly impact their lives, which will only worsen by a unidimensional pursuit of GDP-based 'progress'. Similarly, suppose an organisation facing a lull in innovation activity conducts a design study. In that case, it may find that its employees are demotivated as they speak of a top-down 'culture' where employees feel overworked and have hardly any slack or psychological safety for innovation and tinkering.

Our intention as design thinkers must be to identify both proximate factors that drive a phenomenon and the deeper, more ultimate factors. Proximate factors are like muscle cramps—issues that should be immediately addressed in the short term, while ultimate factors are like a good lifestyle and diet that address the underlying causes and need a longer commitment.

Issue: Urban heat islands
Proximate factor: Lack of shade or trees
Ultimate factor: Global warming

Issue: Less innovation in business
Proximate factor: Stressful work environment, no slack
Ultimate factor: Low emotional quotient and poor communication skills of managers as the business model is built around maximising the 'utilisation rate' of workers.

5. Make strategic decisions identifying actions

The strategic design thinking process can provide urgent (short-term) and long-term actionable points. The simple Eisenhower Matrix, named after the US president and military general Dwight Eisenhower, can be helpful in everyday decision-making. The strategic design thinking process can help design thinkers identify important and urgent actionable points.

	Urgent	Not urgent
Important	DO	PLAN
Not important	DELEGATE	DELETE

The matrix suggests that urgent and important tasks must be addressed first, while important but non-urgent tasks must be planned in advance. Urgent tasks which are non-important should be delegated to others, while non-urgent, non-important tasks should be deleted. Once the urgency and importance have been determined using the principles of design thinking, action can be taken after placing them in the matrix to chart an order of priority.

Design Thinking Dashboard

How could the design thinking approach have helped in the cases of COVID-19 and Teflon? Think of design thinking as a dashboard that gives leaders visibility about the needs, wants, desires, issues, and asks of various stakeholders—visible, invisible, heard and unheard.

If implemented in health systems like Wuhan or large organisations like DuPont, the dashboard would include stakeholders like Wuhan doctors and DuPont employees. The dashboard would open a door for atypical voices to be heard. Consequently, early warnings from doctors in Wuhan during the pandemic or the lab reports from 3M about C8 in the 1960s would not be ignored.

For typical and atypical stakeholders to be heard consistently and for their needs, wants, desires, issues and asks to be continuously engaged with, we need a strategic design thinking process to be integrated into the routines of the organisations, where stakeholder maps are iteratively developed, improved upon, engaged with and used to identify important and urgent action points.

In a world where data analysis is an essential but no longer a challenging skill in our complex world, the new challenging skill is being an empathetic design thinker who can listen in time to both—the typicals and the atypicals—and learn from their stories.

***Value ~~intellect~~ empathy*:**

- Crises emerge when stakeholders are systematically ignored.
- Data generation is slow and biased by power, so stories are essential for motivating action.
- Empathy through immersive listening is an essential skill for understanding stories.
- The strategic design thinking process uses immersive listening to understand systems.
- So, immersive design thinking can create resilient systems.

Rule 1

LEAD FROM THE ~~TOP~~ GROUND

'As much as possible, get the opinions of the people who are actually doing the work.'[14]

—Taiichi Ohno, father of the Toyota Production System

1

Strategy 101: Inimitable Capabilities

Strategic organisations outperform the industry by developing inimitable capabilities.

WHAT makes some organisations more successful than others? We live in a world where no two people are the same. The art of bringing people together, 'the science of association', is at the heart of all progress. Business too is conducted in organisations, and organisations are at their core about *organising* people and processes to pursue and execute set or emergent goals.

To understand what lies at the foundation of successful organisations, let us brush up on basic MBA-level strategy that is taught in class so that we are familiar with some core concepts. We can then build upon these concepts.[15]

Strategy is the art of identifying which goals the organisation must focus on from multiple options and how. The aim of business often tends to be maximising long-term profits, which are determined by various factors. We will discuss two central factors: industry structure and capabilities.

Industry Influences Performance

Not all industries are equally profitable. Some industries, like the soft drinks industry dominated by Coca-Cola and Pepsi, which every MBA student knows of, are more profitable than other industries, like the airline industry, where bankruptcies are all too common (from Kingfisher Airlines to Jet Airways).

Industry and its structure are critical factors shaping business outcomes. When analysing an industry, looking at its supply/value chain helps us understand its structure and profitability. Members of an industry's value chain—suppliers, buyers, entrants and rivals—play a vital role in determining the nature of an industry and the level of profits the industry can sustain.

Porter's Forces

Here is a list of checkpoints to look for when analysing an industry.

- *Is it too easy to enter an industry due to low entry barriers?*

Such an 'attractive' industry, like the airline industry, may counterintuitively be unprofitable due to high levels of competition.

- *Is rivalry in the industry price war, or have rival businesses found a niche (differentiation) for themselves?*

If an industry has price wars, like in the retail industry, profits will be marginal. Industries where rivals have found niches, like in the electronics industry, can sustain more profits.

- *Does the industry have powerful buyers or suppliers?*

Industries like auto-components manufacturing with powerful buyers (automotive giants) or suppliers are unlikely to sustain profits as they have low bargaining power.

- *Are there substitutes for the industry's product?*

Having a substitute for the product, such as the railways in Europe, which can substitute for airlines, can erode the industry's profitability.[16]

The stage of an industry also affects levels of profit. Here are a few typical stages an industry goes through in its life cycle.

In the early stage, the market is nascent, and product innovation in the industry is essential. Different versions of the same product exist, each trying to sell their vision of the product to the customers. Consider the nascent smartphone industry of the 2000s, which had many concept designs of smartphones, from Blackberry to Palm Treo to Nokia N.

The industry then moves to the growth stage, where businesses that succeed in process innovation can operate at scale, and industry standards get set. In the smartphone industry, a design standard was established after the introduction of the Apple iPhone, which brought the multitouch screen format to the smartphone. It formed alliances with telecom providers to reduce ownership and internet usage costs.

The growth stage, where industry standards are set, leads to shakeouts, where many rivals exit the business as they fail to adapt to the industry standards. In the 2010s, the smartphone industry entered a stage of a shakeout. From multiple mobile operating systems like Symbian, Windows Mobile and Blackberry OS, the number of operating systems declined to two: Apple iOS and Google Android.

After the shakeout, the industry enters a mature stage with a few dominant businesses (technology giants) remaining. As an industry matures, there may be limited returns from product or process innovation, and businesses may be inclined to pursue anti-competitive 'dirty' strategies. Today, there is greater scrutiny from antitrust regulators like the European Union, the US Congress, and India's Competition Commission over the strategies pursued by tech giants. For example, countries are debating how these firms should use user data and if these companies' current business model is creating a surveillance system.

Mature industries often stagnate until they are disrupted by creative destruction, where a new set of players introduces a product that fulfils customer needs with a distinctly different and creative approach, not followed by incumbent businesses that are set in their ways.

Just like the smartphone industry disrupted the traditional mobile telecom industry, in the 2020s, artificial intelligence (AI) promises to disrupt the smartphone industry. New or previously small players like DeepMind (whose work even won its co-founder and researcher the 2024 Nobel Prize in Chemistry), OpenAI and Nvidia have already made a big splash in the industry, while incumbent big tech businesses like Apple, Google, Intel and Microsoft form alliances and do acquisitions to follow the leads generated by these new players.

Significant disruptions such as the internet revolution and AI often disrupt not just one but multiple industries. For example, AI challenges not just the smartphone business but also IT giants based in India. However, it is not always necessary that old companies fail with the rise of new ones. With careful adoption and upgradation of new *capabilities*, businesses can survive and thrive in new environments. IBM, founded in 1911, is a good example of this, as it consistently expanded to new markets, inventing technologies such as the ATM, floppy disk, hard disk drive, SQL programming language and the barcode. Can it survive the AI revolution as well? A lot will depend on IBM's capabilities.

Capabilities Bring Strategic Advantage

Analysing the industry helps us understand its general profitability levels. However, within the same industry, some businesses, like Indian airline company Indigo, outperform others based on their unique, strategically valuable and inimitable capabilities. For example, Indigo's operational efficiency, which has developed over several years since its founding, offers unique cost advantages that other airline companies cannot easily replicate. The development of these capabilities is often path-dependent on history, taking years to mature.

> *What resources and capabilities should the business develop in-house, and what should it outsource?*
>
> This is a central question in strategy and a major strategic decision that cannot be made overnight. Businesses compete for capabilities (like developing capabilities in AI). Sometimes, they do *mergers and acquisitions* (e.g., Google acquiring DeepMind). At other times, they do *partnerships* (e.g., Microsoft and Apple partnering with OpenAI) or *joint ventures* (e.g., Starbucks and Tata) to learn new capabilities. Some work (e.g., Google's acquisition of YouTube), and others do not (e.g., Microsoft's acquisition of Nokia).

Price and cost are two levers businesses can pull to compete in the market. In certain industries, such as discount retail or airlines, prices are set by broader market forces. Hence, businesses build capabilities that can drive down costs to succeed. Indigo has successfully developed operational capabilities that help the company run at low cost, as their original tagline said, 'On time'.

Multinational retailer Walmart is a famed business known for its 'cost leadership' and frugal operations. Its rival, e-commerce giant Amazon, has also been able to dominate online retail with similar cost leadership. Strategic decisions about store/warehouse location and investments in IT and inventory management have given these retail giants the scale, organisation and agility with which they can achieve superior low-cost operations.

In other industries, price and willingness to pay can be altered by offering new product features (e.g., in the smartphone industry), building an attractive brand (e.g., luxury brands), or creating a good ecosystem (e.g., Microsoft). Businesses that attempt to raise the willingness-to-pay of customers are called differentiators. Technology giant Apple is a dominant differentiator with the tagline 'Think different'. It has developed inimitable hardware and software integration capabilities, a well-curated ecosystem and a resourceful supply chain. It has deployed these resources to create a brand that can uniquely produce premium products at scale.

Businesses are usually advised against aiming for both cost leadership and differentiation. It is often difficult to have low costs and demand a high premium from customers. Why is being a jack of all trades not a good idea? Because pursuing any strategy requires a specialised set of activities, and pursuing an 'I want it all' strategy often forces businesses into activities that are not compatible with each other. Consider Indigo. The capabilities that deliver the low-cost strategy of Indigo are incompatible with the capabilities required to be a premium Indian airline like Vistara (now absorbed into Air India). Both should ideally not try to tread into each other's domain, as they are not good at the other's business model. When erstwhile premium airline companies Jet Airways and Kingfisher attempted to do both, they went bankrupt.

Inimitable capabilities are a source of sustained competitive advantage for businesses. These are often difficult to point out, as they are held in the complex social dynamics between the organisation's different stakeholders. This is why it may be challenging for another business, no matter how dominant, to replicate the capabilities of a business such as Indigo or Apple.

2

Capabilities Lie in Relationships

Inimitable capabilities are embedded in the relational contracts and trust between stakeholders.

WHERE do the capabilities of organisations lie? Let us take a look inside organisations to answer this. All stakeholders, even those within an organisation, have unique needs, wants, desires, issues and asks. The unique incentives and concerns of an organisation's stakeholders can create a social dynamic of either cooperation or conflict, shaping how effective organisations are in producing process improvements and product innovations, which lie at the heart of successful organisations.

The Worker-centrism of the Toyota Production System

Consider you are the manager of an automobile manufacturing plant. You interact with the various stakeholders of the plant, such as the line worker, production manager, supplier, and so on. All of these can have different concerns. A line worker who finds a pattern that might lead to defects in the product may face a dilemma—

should they raise the alarm and stop production? The worker may wonder: 'Should I raise the alarm when I see a problem, or will I be blamed for raising concerns about trivial things and causing losses?' A production manager who sometimes responds to false alarms may wonder: 'Are issues raised by workers sincere concerns, or are these tactics to cut corners and be less productive?'

Similarly, a supplier has to decide whether to dedicate their resources fully to a large automobile manufacturer or to serve multiple businesses. They may wonder: 'Can I invest in a long-term relationship with this particular manufacturer, or should I explore alternative options, just in case?' An HR person at the company may similarly wonder: 'Whose demands are more legitimate—the management's efficiency objectives or the issues raised by workers?'

As the manager, how can you manage the different concerns in your manufacturing plant? A delicate balance of trust is at the heart of even the most massive and efficient engineering systems like the legendary Toyota Production System (TPS). At the heart of TPS and its lean manufacturing philosophy is *Kaizen* or 'continuous improvement', which rests on the ability of all employees, most importantly line workers, to identify defects and stop the line if they spot potential errors. Any worker can stop the production line when they spot an error so that defects do not flow across the entire production line.

Workers at Toyota factories are empowered to be hands-on problem-solvers in the factory line, continuously improving the processes by themselves and not waiting for a supervisor's permission. The father of the Toyota Production System, Taiichi Ohno, summarised this philosophy of worker-driven continuous improvement by saying, 'Something is wrong if workers do not look around each day, find things that are tedious or boring, and then rewrite the procedures. Even last month's manual should be out of date.'[17]

For such a system to work, supervisors must trust the workers that the concerns they raise are genuine and not excuses. There must be a culture of 'respect for people' from the top to the bottom of the organisation's hierarchy. Continuous improvement and respect for people are the two pillars of the 'Toyota Way', considered the most legendary manufacturing system of the twentieth century.

The Toyota System works when this trust works, and stakeholder beliefs and norms are aligned. The Toyota line worker does not worry if the supervisor will question their motives, and a supervisor feels confident that line workers will raise alarms sincerely. Similarly, suppliers feel confident investing in long-term processes dedicated to serving Toyota, which helps the company maintain zero inventory of components and minimal delivery time from suppliers, keeping the manufacturing plant lean. Similarly, HR does not feel a tension between the management's goals and workers' concerns, as the management's stated and sincerely held approach, the Toyota Way, is to listen to those doing the production. Genuine emphasis on harmonious and trustworthy relationships is the key.

When this trust between different stakeholders crumbles, systems malfunction too. Maintaining this balance is one of the managers' most challenging tasks, because such trust does not emerge through written contractual arrangements but through the long-term nurturing of a culture where all stakeholders understand their roles and expectations and feel fairly treated and heard.

We call such tacit aspects of exchange relationships *relational contracts*, which work through uncodified norms and beliefs. Exporting these norms and beliefs from one place to another is complex, so even the best-designed systems may fail when established in the wrong place. Capabilities of businesses are often embedded in these relational contracts between different stakeholders of the business.

Apple's Collaborative Culture of Innovation

Developing or acquiring capabilities is a challenging task for businesses. Like process improvements in manufacturing systems, product innovation at companies like Apple also rests on the ability of various stakeholders to trust each other so that ideas can be exchanged without hesitation, promoting collaboration, which is at the heart of innovation.

The Investment Dilemma

Almost every relationship, at a given time, has trust asymmetry—where one party (principal) must trust while the other party (agent) must be trustworthy. In such situations, the common (equilibrium) outcome tends to be where the principal cannot trust the agent, and hence, no investment gets done, leading to lost opportunities. When such relationships can be repeated between the same principal and agent, trust and no trust can be potential outcomes depending on how players play the game. Relational contracts are an understanding where the principal and agent establish trust through a repeated history of cooperation.

A junior engineer at an R&D institution may not be willing to trust their superiors if they believe their ideas will not be rewarded in the organisation, or worse, will be stolen by someone else, who will take credit for them.

Many innovation cultures get ruined by mistrust, where juniors cannot trust their seniors to give them the due credit for their efforts. Hence, in such dysfunctional systems, ideas are not exchanged.

It takes time and a repeated history of trust and trustworthy behaviour for a stable ecosystem to emerge, where various stakeholders can trust and be trustworthy to each other. In such stable ecosystems, stakeholders can invest in creating inimitable business capabilities.

Consider Apple and its ability to create innovation at scale. Apple co-founder and former CEO Steve Jobs said about its innovation culture, 'We're paying people to tell us what to do. I don't view that we pay people to do things. That's easy—to find people to do things. What's harder is to find people to tell you what should be done.'[18] A culture that values a bottom-up idea generation leads to flat organisational structures, the hallmark of modern innovative companies.

Such a culture of collaboration sharply contrasts with many hierarchical organisations where the writ of egoistic managers runs large. Such hierarchical organisations may not be in a position to drive serendipitous innovation. However, hierarchical organisations, like space agencies, may still be able to deliver well on well-specified innovation missions.

Tim Cook on Apple's Culture

Apple's CEO Tim Cook in 2013, delving deeper into Apple's culture of collaboration, said:

> You look for wicked smart people. You look for people who appreciate different points of view. People who care enough that they have an idea at 11 at night and they want to call and talk to you about it. Because they're so excited about it, they want to push the idea further. And that they believe that somebody can help them push the idea another step instead of them doing everything themselves.
>
> I've never met anyone in my life, maybe they exist, that could do something so incredible by themselves in companies with global footprints. In our world, in Apple's world, the reason Apple is special is we focus on hardware, software, and services. And the magic happens where those three come together.

> And so, it's unlikely that somebody that's focused on one of those in and of itself can come up with magic and so you want people collaborating in such a way so you can produce these things that can't be produced otherwise. And you want people to believe in that.[19]

If a business attempts to replicate Toyota's manufacturing system or Apple's innovation capabilities, they must first replicate the relational contracts that underpin these organisations. In these contracts, a unique history and social dynamics have enabled these businesses to create environments where stakeholders feel incentivised to invest in developing new process or product innovations.

Even if Toyota or Apple wrote a detailed handbook on how they worked, their systems may not be replicable simply because the historical and cultural context may differ from one organisation to another. Each organisation would have to figure out its own way. How can organisations develop their own unique ways in which trustworthy relationships can be established between different stakeholders? The Tatas can show the way.

3

Nurturing Trust in Organisations

Nurturing trust with stakeholders needs long-term commitment and is immensely valuable.

WHY should nurturing good relationships be difficult if they are so important? Various factors tempt organisations to exploit their connections rather than nurture them.

In the previous chapter, we learnt that capabilities are essential for the success of organisations, and truly inimitable capabilities are embedded in the relational contracts between different stakeholders of the organisation. Good collaborative relationships between stakeholders help develop better processes and product innovation—a natural question arises: How can businesses nurture such collaborative relationships?

Tata's Grounded Leadership

India's largest conglomerate, the Tata Group, founded by Jamsetji Tata in 1868, can offer an example.[20] In an era marked by the ruthless, profit-driven ethos of robber-baron capitalism in the West, the Tatas built an organisation prioritising its stakeholders' welfare. J.R.D. Tata, later chairman, articulated this philosophy succinctly: 'The Tata philosophy of management has always been, and is today more than ever, that corporate enterprises must be managed not merely in the interests of their owners, but equally in those of their employees, of the consumers of their products, of the local community and finally of the country as a whole.'[21]

One of the first enterprises of Jamsetji Tata was a textile mill, Empress Mills, established in 1877 at a time when Indian textiles had declined due to colonialism. Jamsetji strategically located the mill in Nagpur, Maharashtra, close to cotton farms, gaining cost advantages. However, he found hiring and retaining factory workers in the largely agrarian town of Nagpur difficult. Factories traditionally were unpleasant places to work—noisy, smoky, sweaty and cramped. Why should someone join such a place when there are other jobs in more pleasant environments?

To address this challenge and to attract workers and increase their motivation, Jamsetji took a constructive approach—he offered some of the most progressive welfare, work and safety policies to workers, which were unheard of at the time.

The late nineteenth century was a time of peak industrialisation in Europe and the USA, and exploitation of workers was rampant. This was the reason behind the eventual rise of labour movements in these regions. Even Indian businesses of the time, following the lead of the West, were no different. But, Jamsetji was far ahead of the times, offering workers benefits like shorter working hours, well-ventilated workspaces and pension and provident funds. He also introduced accident compensation and free medical aid, showcasing a deep commitment to the well-being of his employees. Most of these policies eventually became global norms enshrined in government legal systems, but the Tatas pioneered these systems ahead of time.

Such grounded leadership was again shown when the Tatas, led by Jamsetji's son Dorabji, established the first steel plant in India, Tata Steel, in 1907 (initially called TELCO), located in a remote but mineral-rich region of what is now Jharkhand. Building a steel plant, Asia's first, in the middle of a dense forest, was no easy feat and required years of surveying in the rugged terrains of the Chotanagpur plateau.

Building such a steel plant was one of the dreams of Jamsetji Tata, and he left specific instructions to his son about the kind of place he wanted to build, 'Be sure to lay wide streets planted with shady trees, every other of a quick-growing variety. Be sure that there is plenty of space for lawns and gardens. Reserve large areas for football, hockey and parks. Earmark areas for Hindu temples, Mohammedan mosques and Christian churches.'[22]

The industrial town that emerged around Tata Steel was Jamshedpur, named after Jamsetji, and it matched Jamsetji's vision, seen as a benchmark in modern industrial town planning. Jamshedpur today is the most populous city of Jharkhand and a harbinger of industrialisation and education.

The company instituted worker-friendly rules, notably introducing the eight-hour workday in 1912. Other follow-up policies included free medical aid in 1915, leave with pay, provident fund and accident compensation schemes in 1920, maternity benefit in 1928, profit sharing in 1934 and a gratuity scheme in 1937, all instituted before India's independence (1947), in the absence of formal regulations.

These labour-friendly policies, especially the 1912 eight-hour workday, implemented at a giant manufacturing institution, the first one in Asia, was unprecedented at the time. It helped Tata attract workers, engineers and professionals to a location that would have been otherwise unattractive for many, creating a cosmopolitan town in the middle of the Chotanagpur forests.

The Tatas During Crises

During times of crisis, the Tatas showed genuine commitment to stakeholders in the 1920s. After the boom in steel demand during World War I, the 1920s were struggling years for Tata Steel, with the company on the verge of shutting its doors. However, Tata's chairman, Dorabji, took exemplary steps, putting his personal assets for sale. His wife Meherbai pawned her jewels for funds, ensuring no worker got their salary late even in such difficult times.

Tata's Forward-looking Stewardship

The unprecedented nature of Tata's labour policies must be appreciated within the broader context of the global labour movement. Since the latter half of the nineteenth century, rapid industrialisation and poor working conditions gave rise to powerful labour movements in the West that demanded better worker conditions. These movements led to the rise of 'labour' parties in the early 1900s in industrialised democratic nations.

For example, the UK's Labour Party emerged during this period, and working men, who previously did not hold property and thus lacked voting rights, eventually won the right to vote in 1918 in the UK. Women won the right to vote in 1928 through a women's rights movement, which was closely associated with the labour movements of the late nineteenth century and later.

Parallel to the labour movements in democratic countries was the rise of the Communist movement, which became a formidable force, especially after overthrowing the Russian Empire in the Russian Revolution of 1917 and forming the USSR. The eight-hour workday became a rallying call for these labour unions and movements, symbolising the fight for better working conditions and workers' rights.

The establishment of the International Labour Organization (ILO) in 1919, at the end of World War I, marked a significant milestone in the global labour movement. One of the ILO's first resolutions was the call for an eight-hour workday and a forty-hour workweek. However, this resolution was only adopted as a legal norm across various nations later. In many industrialised economies, most labour reforms, including the implementation of the eight-hour workday, were reactions to these structural changes driven by strong labour movements and political pressure from emerging labour parties.

India, not an industrialised nation in the early twentieth century, lacked a significant labour movement comparable to the West. While there were agrarian movements during this period, industrial labour unrest was minimal. Unlike in the West, where businesses often reacted to labour unrest and political changes, the Tata Group in India was not responding to such pressures. Instead, their approach was markedly forward-looking. They proactively understood the importance of worker conditions, learning from global developments.

The Tata Group showed a keen interest in labour welfare, even supporting research. In the 1910s, Tata supported labour welfare studies at the newly instituted London School of Economics, emphasising their commitment to improving worker conditions. Tata Steel's introduction of the eight-hour workday in 1912 was a testament to this proactive approach. This policy was implemented well before the ILO's resolution and without the impetus of labour strikes or unrest, largely absent in India's pre-industrial context.

The labour movement was at the foundation of the emerging American dream—a dream where any working-age person hopes to get a steady, dignified job at a respectful organisation that pays them enough to raise a family, buy a house, educate and support their children and retire comfortably, with good opportunities for career progression at the organisation. Organisations like the American automobile manufacturers Ford and General Motors, in cities like the automotive manufacturing city of Detroit, were the heart of this dream, as they offered stable, well-paying jobs with dignified work hours.

If there were to be an equivalent Indian dream, what would it be? The town of Jamshedpur, fondly called Tatanagar, could offer a model. Unique to the vision of the Tatas was their sense of responsibility that did not extend only towards their employees but also to their families. That is why, right from the earliest days of the establishment of Jamshedpur, the Tatas not only invested in building the steel plant and the health, safety, working and life conditions of their employees, but also the education and welfare of their families. To be an attractive organisation, Tata Steel needed to attract talent from across the country, who would only move to the remote Chotanagpur plateau if they could see a pathway to a good life for themselves and their families.

Creating a town that offered a good life to the employees and their families was a daring enterprise, and to do so, Tata Steel established a special town services division in 1911. There were several critics of Tata's approach, which not only focused on manufacturing steel but also on building a city around it. To this accusation, Ratanji Dadabhoy Tata, the director of Tata Steel, said in 1923, 'We are constantly accused by people of wasting money in the town of Jamshedpur. We are asked why it should be necessary to spend so much on housing, sanitation, roads, hospitals and on welfare ... Gentlemen, people who ask these questions are sadly lacking in imagination. We are not putting up a row of workmen's huts in Jamshedpur—we are building a city.'[23]

Jamsetji Tata summarised this approach even more succinctly, 'In a free enterprise, the community is not just another stakeholder in business, but is in fact the very purpose of its existence.'[24] True to their purpose, the Tatas established not only multiple businesses but also towns like Jamshedpur and Mithapur, Gujarat (base of Tata Chemicals), as well as building or supporting renowned institutions such as the Indian Institute of Science (IISc), Bangalore,

Tata Institute of Social Sciences (TISS), Tata Memorial Hospital, Tata Institute of Fundamental Research (TIFR) and the National Centre for Performing Arts (NCPA) in Mumbai, and the Xavier Labour Relations Institute (XLRI) in Jamshedpur.

The Tata Brand: A Legacy that Stakeholders Trust

Tata is a business group. Business groups are common in developing countries. Strategy researchers[25] show that such groups enter multiple businesses to develop various capabilities, which would have been easier to buy from the market in a more developed country but not in less developed ones. However, it is rare for business groups to be strong brand names.

Tata is India's largest business conglomerate, but more. It is India's most valuable brand, created over one and a half centuries of stewardship rooted in a deep sense of responsibility towards the community. Tata's brand inspires trust, not just among customers but also employees and the more critical stakeholders. Such a strong brand name helps Tata attract stakeholders beyond customers; people not only want to buy Tata's products but also wish to work and partner with them for both business and social causes.

As India grows its economy, it will inevitably produce global brands, just as post-war developing countries like Japan did with brands like Honda, Nintendo, Nissan, Panasonic, Sony and Toyota; Korea developed brands like Hyundai, Kia and Samsung; Finland developed a brand like Nokia; and China developed brands like Mi, Huawei, Lenovo and Haier, as they grew their economy.

Tata Group is expected to be one of India's breakout global brands. As a business, Tata is strongly positioned to undertake several transformational challenges of the twenty-first century due to its name, which inspires trust and attracts stakeholders. Consider Tata's embrace of alternative energy and its 'UniEVerse' strategy. Tata Motors is at the forefront of electric (EV) car production and sales in India, selling more EV cars than any competitors. Similarly, Tata Power is aggressively at the forefront of embracing renewable fuel as a source of electricity and hopes to create a chain of EV charging stations across India, which shall promote the adoption of EV vehicles. Tata Chemicals similarly hopes to be at the forefront of battery development and production in the country.

Tata may be one of many conglomerates with multiple business interests. Still, the trust in its brand name attracts a critical mass of customers, talented engineers, managers, workers and component suppliers in a way that other conglomerates may not. Tata does the same when entering businesses like aviation, where it uses its strengths in different sectors like hospitality and FMCG to deliver differentiated aviation services. The name becomes an attractor, leveraging its stakeholder-centric approach to its advantage to enter new financially attractive opportunities.

For a business, Tata's brand position is enviable, where the organisation's name attracts stakeholders willing to go along with its vision(s). Organisations must show genuine commitment and respect towards stakeholders over decades to build such a trusted name. For example, in 2008, after Tata's iconic Taj Hotel in Mumbai faced deadly terrorist attacks on 26 November, the Tata Group took exemplary steps for the welfare of those employees' families who died in the attacks. Tata's chairman, Ratan Tata, personally visited each victim's family and paid them the salaries they would have received in their entire lifetime.[26]

4

From the Ground to the C-Suite

We live in times of transactional relationships, where organisations hold narrow focus.

JAMSHEDPUR became the foundation for many industrial towns in India, several of them in east India itself, like Bhilai in Chhattisgarh, Bokaro in Jharkhand, Durgapur in West Bengal, and Kalinganagar (recent) and Rourkela in Odisha. Similarly, cities like Detroit and Pittsburgh represented industrial hubs in the United States, supporting large working-class populations and their transition to middle-class incomes. Companies like Ford and General Motors were generous employers. The years between the 1920s and the 1970s could be called a period of stakeholderism, where labour rights were central, and the workers' voices were considered crucial, just as indispensable as the voices of shareholders. Labour unions were powerful stakeholders. What happened to that era?

Stakeholderism vs Shareholderism

The 1980s heralded a new view on the economy, now called the era of shareholder primacy. As incomes and wages grew with a rising middle class in the West, the cost of labour grew as well, and this led to rising prices or diminishing margins in manufacturing for businesses. Powerful labour unions in the West would call strikes and bargain hard with the management (representing shareholders) for a higher share of overall profits.

Countries like Japan since the 1960s, and then China since the 1980s, in contrast, became increasingly adept at manufacturing, and the manufacturing industries of the West began to migrate East, worried by rising labour costs at home. While Japan followed a more quality-centric approach to manufacturing (e.g., the Toyota Production System), China (ironically a Communist state) allowed the creation of sweatshop-like factories where workers had significantly fewer rights and were willing to work at significantly lower wages, low enough to offset expenses like transportation.

Pursuing profit to benefit shareholders became the primary goal—the objective was to maximise revenue and lower costs. These efficiency-enhancing decisions aimed at 'optimisation' were often made in the C-suite, often by technocratic men (typically with an MBA) with minimal knowledge of the ground.

Businesses outsourced their operations to low-cost locations, reducing the responsibilities they used to have towards workers. Erstwhile manufacturing cities like Detroit became desolate in a few decades, and Chinese cities grew in their place. Millions of good, stable potential jobs were lost in the West, and hundreds of millions were lifted out of poverty in China.

A new organisational form also began to emerge in the West. In place of manufacturing plants that resembled a city, flat and porous organisations emerged in the West in regions like Silicon Valley, which proved to be highly agile and innovative. A new understanding of career developed, where professionals did not spend their entire careers in a single organisation and switched jobs frequently, pollinating expertise and ideas across organisations. With such a view on career and business, organisations too became absolved of treating their employees like 'family', and relationships became more transactional rather than community-oriented.

As the stakeholderism of the early twentieth century gave way to shareholderism of the late twentieth century, it sparked a fervent debate—which was better? It would be too simplistic to say that the poor preferred the former and the rich preferred the latter. Stakeholderism prioritises long-term stability, ethical practices and widespread benefits, while shareholderism focuses on immediate returns, rapid growth and competitive advantages, albeit with higher risks and potential ethical compromises. Each approach has pros and cons, impacting various stakeholders in different ways, summarised in the table below.

	On-the-ground stakeholderism	**C-suite shareholderism**
Employees	Job security and welfare, *but* slower wage growth. Preferred by employees valuing job stability and ethical practices.	Opportunities for higher wages and rapid advancement, *but* lower job security. Preferred by ambitious and career-driven individuals.
Investors	Sustainable long-term returns, *but* lower immediate returns. Preferred by socially responsible and long-term investors.	High potential returns, *but* higher risk and volatility. Preferred by high-risk tolerance and short-term investors.

	On-the-ground stakeholderism	**C-suite shareholderism**
Customers	Focus on quality and service, *but* higher costs. Preferred by ethically conscious consumers.	Competitive pricing, *but* possible quality compromises. Preferred by price-sensitive consumers, mass market.
Business partners	Long-term partnerships based on trust, *but* less flexibility. Preferred by long-term suppliers, strategic partners.	Flexibility to adapt quickly, *but* unstable relationships. Preferred by agile suppliers, opportunistic partners.
Communities	Positive CSR impact, *but* slower economic transformation. Preferred by community leaders.	Rapid job creation, *but* potential neglect of community welfare. Preferred by local entrepreneurs.
Innovation	Ethical and sustainable, *but* slow innovation. Preferred by industries like healthcare, green tech.	Fast-paced, competitive innovations, *but* ethical risks. Preferred by tech startups, aggressive growth sectors.
Economic growth	Broad-based *but* slow growth. Preferred by groups desiring equitable distribution of resources.	Rapid *but* inequality-inducing growth. Preferred by groups desiring allocation of resources to the most productive.

Stakeholderism *and* Shareholderism

The choice between a stakeholder- and shareholder-centric approach may seem like a dilemma—the former appears to be a more relational approach, while numbers, efficiency and optimisation drive the other.

However, the two approaches are not dichotomous if we look at some of the most successful and respected contemporary organisations. For example, Toyota achieved superior quality, zero defects, high reliability and competitive prices for customers by prioritising worker empowerment in its plants and long-term relationships with suppliers, building zero inventory lean manufacturing plants. Similarly, Starbucks, the world's largest coffeehouse chain, grew by developing sustainable and high-quality supply chain linkages between customers and coffee farmers and an attractive working environment for their baristas, whom they call 'partners'. FMCG giant Unilever has taken a similar stakeholder-centric approach, which has made sustainability and ethical sourcing the core competency of its business.

Businesses like Toyota, Starbucks, and Unilever have turned their strong relational contracts with their stakeholders, nurtured over decades, like the Tatas, into inimitable capabilities that also increase shareholder value. All these companies, including the Tatas, are strong financial performers.

A more pragmatic way to think about this debate around stakeholderism and shareholderism is to recognise that *stakeholderism brings inimitable capabilities for organisations, generating value for shareholders in the long run*. Since the 1980s, labour movements have significantly weakened, but other movements, such as the environmental movements, have grown. Many businesses like DuPont focus on the short term, lacking a broad vision for their organisation. Such organisations are often reactive to these stakeholder movements, caring about these stakeholders only when pressure is put on them. However, businesses with a purpose and a vision, like the Tatas, are proactive, and working with stakeholders is central to their long-term strategy of creating maximum value for shareholders.

Maybe money can be made in both ways—through blind hustle for profit or conscious nurturing of people and the planet. Only the latter is suitable for a burning planet.

5

Leading with a Himalayan Mindset

True leadership is not a position, but a mindset of utmost engagement and empathy.

GOOD organisations attract skilled people who accentuate, build and nurture their capabilities. Skilled people do not wait to be told what to do or for a position where they can finally showcase leadership. Leadership is not a position at the top, to be attained one day. It is an everyday mindset. Do you have a leader's mindset?

Organisations can create a culture where people are of two types: the *evasive* or *engagement type*. In evasive organisations, only some, if any, have a leadership mindset. Instead, a culture exists of being 'yes men' or victims, not agents of change. DuPont showcased this culture of evasion when no one took responsibility for their products and got away with Teflon poisoning. In such organisations, even those who fill leadership positions tend to be more like a 'boss' than a leader.

In engagement-type organisations, people have a mindset of leadership, which is diffused in the organisation's culture and incentives, where each employee is called upon to be an agent of change. Such organisations can be said to have deep reservoirs of leadership. In such organisations, all employees are expected to be leaders, and those called upon positions of leadership are not the 'boss'. Toyota and Apple showcase this culture well, where their workers and engineers are agents of change, and the organisation's success depends entirely on their grounded actions.

Professional armies show this engagement mindset and a culture of diffused leadership well. 'Lead by example' is a prominent principle. Army professionals cultivate a culture of leadership, where they take responsibility and do not wait for others or someone superior to take charge. Each army officer must be ready to take charge and act decisively. Army professionals are disciplined and respectful of a chain of command but are not mere followers.

India's legendary Field Marshal Sam Manekshaw, credited with building the foundations of a modern professional army in India, said the following about these two mindsets. About the evasive mindset, he said, 'A Yes Man is a dangerous man. He is a menace. He will go very far. He can become a minister, a secretary or a Field Marshal but he can never become a leader nor, ever be respected. He will be used by his superiors, disliked by his colleagues and despised by his subordinates. So discard the Yes Man.'[27] Instead, Manekshaw hoped all his soldiers would be leaders. He firmly believed that leadership as a mindset could be cultivated, saying, 'Give me a man or a woman with common sense and who is not an idiot, and I assure you can make a leader out of him or her.'[28]

Organisations in which leadership is honed within all its members are resilient in adversity. Conversely, adversity showcases an organisation's leadership depth, which is only as resilient as its employees. How would evasive organisations respond to adversity? Its employees may flee and jump ship in the first instance of discomfort.

A group of US-based economists, in a 2021 paper,[29] showed that decentralised organisations, where people at the grassroots enjoy more autonomy, can be more resilient during economic downturns. When we think of leadership, we often think of CXOs, boardrooms, and blueprints.[30] When the environment is stable, boardroom leadership can work. First, a blueprint is designed to unite the organisation towards a goal. Second, this blueprint is executed effectively through a suitable organisational structure. However, under highly uncertain situations, blueprint leadership is no longer appropriate.

Under true uncertainty, the contours of the problem are unclear, and there is too much ambiguity for any blueprint or a single 'brilliant' leader to be effective. Leadership under true uncertainty thus needs to be agile and responsive to the most immediate information, as organisations that would be best able to continually adapt to the changing environment will have the best chances at doing well. So, when no blueprint is effective, the focus must be on organisational design and processes that enable grounded action.

The rise of San Francisco's Silicon Valley and its contrast to Boston's Route 128 present an excellent example of the importance of effective organisational design in an ambiguous world. Silicon Valley and Route 128 were technology hubs that sprang from university-based innovation and were supported by post-World War II US military spending.

During the highly uncertain 1980s, when technology began to change rapidly and the contours of future technology and IT businesses were unclear, Silicon Valley thrived while Route 128 declined. Why? AnnaLee Saxenian provided a fascinating insight into this divergence in her 1996 book *Regional Advantage*.[31] While both regions seemed similar on a wide range of parameters, she discovered they were very distinct when she looked at the network structure within and between businesses in Silicon Valley and Route 128. Silicon Valley's loosely linked team structures encouraged autonomy and communication across divisions and organisations. In contrast, Route 128 was dominated by autarkic corporations with rigid boundaries and hierarchies.

While businesses in Silicon Valley allowed for horizontal communication, the communication within businesses in the Route 128 region was vertical. The hierarchical, structured and barricaded organisational structure enabled a more deliberative and planned approach to strategy, suitable for Route 128 businesses in the era of technological and market certainty until the 1970s. However, the same deliberative structure became a bottleneck when the market changed rapidly in the 1980s. In contrast, the agility and adaptability of Silicon Valley businesses became a strategic advantage in an era in which communication mattered more than a blueprint.

Silicon Valley and its continued success showcases the importance of grounded leadership and the need to hone a leadership mindset at the grassroots of organisations, which is a standard recipe for success. Hence, it becomes important that we appreciate a more grounded understanding of leadership.

Push Your Gears, Let Your Acts Inspire Others

Leadership shows under adversity, especially when facing challenges. Apple found itself in such a situation in 1997, when it was on the verge of bankruptcy. Apple's CEO Steve Jobs, who had been unceremoniously fired in 1985 from the organisation he founded, was brought back to the helm. Was it the charismatic leadership that turned Apple around? Not just that.

Charismatic individuals exude a sense of competence and confidence, with which they articulate a vision that brings their organisations together. When an organisation is in shambles and demotivated, such individuals certainly matter. However, delivering turnaround products like the iMac (1998) and iPod (2001), which saved the company's fortunes, required more than just charismatic leadership. It required a team, about which Steve Jobs said, 'The greatest people are self-managing. They don't need to be managed. Once they know what to do, they'll go figure out how to do it ... What they need is a common vision, and that's what leadership is.'[32]

Being charismatic and grounded are not alternatives but vital components of successful leadership. Competence underpins both. Yet, our charismatic flair may get subdued by self-limiting beliefs. We often have certain limiting beliefs about ourselves. 'I am not fit for this job'; 'I am not good enough'; 'I cannot lead'; 'I am good at coding but not at dealing with people'. However, such beliefs are often based on anecdotal experiences or inferences from our life histories. Someone who has never had a chance to lead may think they are not good, even if they can quickly adapt their skills when the right challenge arises. At times, such self-limiting beliefs could be a result of internalised stereotypes, which especially hurts marginalised groups: 'I am gay, so I will never be accepted as a leader', or 'I am a woman, so I cannot be assertive'.

When we do things that are outside our immediate comfort zone, they can be challenging, and our bodies and minds may give us various signals to stop. Think of it from the perspective of a car. A car that has driven only under a speed of 20 km/hour may have only known a single gear, and every time the car is pushed faster, the car may grumble and make sounds, as the first gear is not enough. But we can get stuck in the first gear due to our self-limiting beliefs: 'My car is meant to drive at 20 km/hour, not more.' We may forget to push to higher gears.

This allegory may also be true in life. We often live assuming we have only one gear, usually living far below our full physical and mental potential. We do not push ourselves. We give up at the first instance of discomfort. But when pushed to the limit, our body and mind respond terrifically and change their gear to a higher level.

How many gears do we have? We can only know if we *consistently* challenge ourselves.

The Ten-second Barrier

Finishing the 100-metre sprint in under 10 seconds was considered a significant human limit. It was breached (officially) for the first time in 1968 by US athlete Jim Hanes. In the next twenty years (till 1988), the barrier was breached by four new athletes; in the next twenty years (till 2008), forty-four new athletes, and in the next fifteen years (until 2023), 114 new athletes.

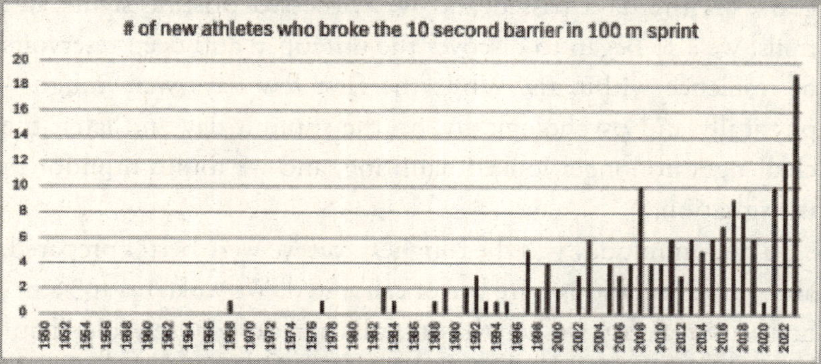

Consider the locals who live in the cold, rugged Himalayan terrain. They possess extraordinary endurance and strength as they adapt to new physical limits. Can we develop endurance and strength like them? Yes, we can; if we do not match them, we can at least go far beyond our baseline. When a challenge meets the right mindset, we can discover that we can gear up and perform beyond our physical, mental and skill limits.

At IIM Bangalore, I took students to the Himalayan Mountain Challenge to teach them about collaborative leadership.[33] My first and most difficult expedition to the Himalayas was in December 2019, where, with a team of students, I trekked to the Kedarkantha peak in waist-deep snow and sub-zero cold as part of the course organised by trekking company India Hikes. Such cold and steep climbs threw us out of our comfort zone as we camped, cooked and survived the three days of ascent and two days of descent. Hierarchies broke down in such adversity, as everyone helped each other. Sometimes, we almost gave up and broke down as we negotiated the harsh cold of the long Himalayan nights.

The first few hours seemed particularly challenging, and so did the first day. At several moments we felt like giving up, feeling unprepared for the mental and physical challenge. But, with the right mindset and some prior training, our body and mind shifted gears. As the days passed and we witnessed pristine sights and trails, we also began to discover the untapped and deep reservoirs of resilience within us. While the first few days were tough—physically and psychologically, on the summit day and later, the challenges no longer looked daunting, and we found humour in the situation.

The summit day was the toughest, yet we were better prepared, and our expectations were better calibrated. We woke up at 3 a.m., had our breakfast, washed the utensils in freezing water, folded our tents and began the steep climb by 5.30 a.m. while it was still dark. This time, the climb, too, seemed more accessible, even though it was steeper. We reached the peak by 10 a.m., climbing faster than on the previous two days.

Once we reached the summit, a dose of adrenaline, released by the sense of achievement and the unadulterated beauty of the Himalayan peaks, overpowered us. We had another challenge—descent—which would take another six hours until we reached our base camp. It was more challenging than expected, putting significant stress on our knees. But, by now, trekking had become fun. Some slid in the snow, others sang along. There were still discomforts. For example, the snow was in our boots, and our feet were freezing. Yet, it all seemed trivial in the face of the adventure.

When we reached the base camp, we pitched our tents and cooked food for a big dinner party. This time, despite the long, cold day, we were more content, not complaining, and enjoying the company and what we had with us. The trek taught us a sage quote often attributed to Edmund Hillary, the first person to climb Mount Everest, 'It is not the mountain we conquer, but ourselves.'[34]

Motivate Big Challenges with Small Wins

The Himalayan Mountain Challenge programme is particularly challenging because of the snow and the windy cold, which is psychologically draining. As the lead of the programme, I have found most noteworthy how different teams handle the situation. A few teams have an unpleasant time, as they become evasive, complain and feel trapped in an unwelcome situation, feeling a sense of victimhood. However, other teams facing the same situation are happy and enthusiastic for most of the trek, and they also have the most collaborative members. These teams are largely randomly allotted, so then what creates the difference? It is the emergent team dynamics.

Pushing the limits is not just about an individual's mindset. Teams make a difference for their members by enabling them, and an individual member can make a difference to their team by being a source of inspiration and motivation. Individuals in engaged teams can push their limits as team members motivate and support each other under adversity, achieving an effect of positive contagion. However, in evasive teams, individuals give up faster, get demotivated and overwhelmed by their problems, often complaining, entering into conflicts and spiralling into negative contagion. Two teams, with minor differences in mindset, can create two contrasting relational contracts within themselves, which then become crucial in determining their success or failure.

Beyond physical endurance, strength and mental capabilities, our psychology significantly impacts our ability to face challenges. When we face psychological discomforts, it does not feel good. But worrying or complaining does not help. Being overwhelmed does not help either. Being in the present helps, as it allows us to respond to uncertainties better. Dividing a long project into small, achievable tasks helps, too.

One can be scientifically grounded when thinking of motivation and pushing the limits under challenging situations. In their 2011 book *The Progress Principle*,[35] Theresa Amabile and Steven Kramer wrote that we should focus on several small wins instead of targeting one big win. Winning motivates us. But it demotivates us when we keep our targets big and spread over long durations and when we fail to fulfil them. In contrast, when we split our targets into smaller achievable wins, such as dividing a long day trail into smaller segments, we achieve 'wins' more often, boosting our motivation.

During a long climb in a harsh environment, each trekking day presents a long psychological journey and needs to be divided into smaller goals so that teams are not overwhelmed. 'Let's have a bite of this snack when we reach the meadows thirty minutes away'; 'Let's take rest at the water point forty-five minutes from now'; 'We have climbed 500 feet up from the last point!'; 'We are just four checkpoints away from the destination'.

At the Kedarkantha trek, whenever we achieved the small goals, no matter how small, it filled us with motivation. Celebrating such small wins boosted the teams' morale. Humour helped, too. Making light of the situation, self-deprecation and a little leg-pulling also worked. Dividing tasks among members helped, too. Everyone does not have to be a pro at technical tasks. Some people offer lively company, which soothes everyone in the team, which is also a vital skill for the organisation's success.

On a trek, you cannot fire your team members. Everyone must reach the destination. Hence, it becomes a remarkable lesson in the leadership of not just bringing people together but also being empathetic and using empathy to understand what the team members need, what they are good at and what would motivate them better—the needs, wants, desires, issues and asks, in the language of design thinking. Teams that manage to get everyone together have a much better time.

The laid-out approach can be encapsulated in what I call 'the Himalayan mindset'. True leadership lies not in titles or positions but in a mindset of utmost engagement, empathy and resilience.

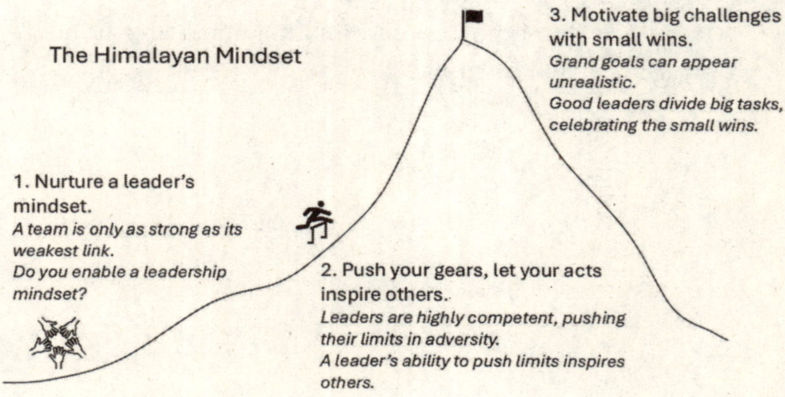

Organisations that embody the Himalayan mindset, such as professional armies, Toyota and Apple, demonstrate the power of distributed leadership and build better relational contracts among the members. In these environments, leadership is not the prerogative of the few but the responsibility of the many. Every member is prepared to step up, take decisive action and adapt to changing circumstances, especially in times of adversity. This decentralised approach ensures that the organisation remains agile, responsive and resilient, qualities that are indispensable in the face of true uncertainty.

***Lead from the ~~top~~ ground*:**

- Strategic organisations outperform the industry by developing inimitable capabilities.
- Inimitable capabilities are embedded in the relational contracts and trust between stakeholders.
- Nurturing trust with stakeholders needs long-term commitment and is immensely valuable.
- But we live in times of transactional relationships, where organisations hold narrow focus.
- True leadership is not a position, but a mindset of utmost engagement and empathy.

Rule 2

PURSUE ~~PROFIT~~ INNOVATION

'Creative destruction is the essential fact about capitalism.'[36]

—Joseph Schumpeter

6

Dirty Strategies

Dirty strategies 'manage' pollution, increase opaqueness and raise barriers to entry to seek rents.

WHEN I was in school, my father taught me a valuable lesson. He explained that there were two ways to succeed in life. He drew two lines, A and B. Let us say we are line A, a 5 cm line, and someone else is line B, our competitor, a 6 cm line. One way to grow is to erase 2 cm from line B. The other way to succeed is to grow 2 cm more. Just like this example, organisations can succeed in two ways: first by raising themselves, and the other by erasing others.

We discussed strategies like that of the Tatas, who try to raise themselves by raising their stakeholders. But for each Tata, there is also a DuPont, which pursues dirty strategies instead.

In business schools, both raising and erasing can be taught as strategies. If the purpose of business is to earn profits, a strategy that is narrowly focused on the profits of the business alone, not considering the broader consequences, could inadvertently be both raising oneself and erasing others. Several examples illustrate how organisations might use dirty strategies that erase others rather than raise themselves.

Managing, Not Eliminating Pollution

One common but dirty approach to strategy is when organisations lobby or conduct other forms of 'networking' to evade the costs associated with negative externalities like pollution. A notable example is DuPont, especially in the way it handled the case of Teflon poisoning.

DuPont engaged in significant lobbying efforts to shape regulatory frameworks (e.g., the US Toxic Substances Control Act) to its advantage, allowing the company to continue using harmful chemicals like C8 without stringent oversight. Similarly, the company operated a 'revolving door' policy with regulatory agencies like the US Environmental Protection Agency (EPA), wherein the company provided plush jobs to regulatory officials, leaving the government in expectation of favourable access (quid pro quo).

The revolving door officials and their valuable networks in the government were often employed to 'manage' regulators through their networks, rather than improve their internal products and processes. For example, during the Teflon poisoning crisis, public scrutiny over the chemical C8 intensified. In 2006, the EPA's Science Advisory Board found C8 to be a toxin. However, DuPont wrote an internal mail to the EPA, directing the body to say the Teflon brand was safe, writing, 'In our opinion, the only voice that can cut through the negative stories, is the voice of EPA. We need EPA ... to quickly (like first thing tomorrow) say the following: Consumer products sold under the Teflon brand are safe.'[37]

The EPA later issued a statement saying, 'The agency does not believe that consumers need to stop using their cookware, clothing, or other stick-resistant, stain-resistant products.'[38] At the end of the

Teflon crisis, the EPA charged a mere $16.5 million to the company for selling a product that brought them billions.

Like DuPont, other polluting companies also conduct similar corporate political actions to reduce the regulatory burdens linked with the adverse effects of their products. For example, fossil fuel-producing companies lobby strongly against regulations that raise taxes on fossil fuel production and consumption. Many of these giant businesses have also been associated with promoting think tanks and politicians that engage in climate denialism.

An example of such a think tank is the Global Climate Coalition (GCC),[39] founded in 1989. The GCC was composed of major corporations and trade associations from the fossil fuel industry and played a significant role in lobbying against international climate agreements and national climate policies. For example, during the negotiations of the 1997 Kyoto Protocol, a landmark international treaty on climate change under the United Nations, the GCC actively lobbied the US government to reject the treaty, arguing that it would harm the economy and be unfair to developed countries. Additionally, the coalition funded public relations campaigns that cast doubt on the scientific consensus regarding climate change, aiming to delay regulatory actions that would impose stricter environmental standards on its member companies. It was eventually disbanded in 2002, once its credibility was severely tarnished as a global scientific consensus emerged about the reality and harms of climate change.

Large internet businesses also lobby against regulations that protect user privacy. For example, consider the so-called European Privacy Association, a European lobbying group with the stated goal of enhancing data protection and internet freedom that instead promotes anti-privacy laws to protect the interests of businesses that leverage user data. Founded in 2009 as a 'think tank', the association did not reveal information about its corporate donors. However, it was ultimately revealed in 2013 that the then internet giants like Microsoft, Google and Yahoo were among its backers. The European Privacy Association has become an example of 'astroturfing', i.e., a practice of making an organisation appear as if it originates from the grassroots but is supported by corporations, politicians, religious or other groups with vested interests that remain hidden.[40]

Increasing, Not Decreasing Opaqueness

Another way organisations try to protect their profits or promote their businesses is by being opaque about the quality and effects of their products. One example of such a dirty strategy is the US tobacco industry's efforts to lobby against smoking hazard warnings. For decades, companies like Philip Morris have engaged in aggressive lobbying and PR campaigns to prevent or weaken regulations requiring health warnings on cigarette packaging. Despite overwhelming evidence of the harmful effects of smoking, these companies prioritised profits over public health, delaying critical health warnings that could save lives.

The food industry is also guilty of such strategies. For example, 'fresh' fruit juices sold by major FMCG companies may market their products with labels and images that feature fresh fruits, hinting that the beverages are made from pure fruit juice. However, a closer inspection of the ingredient list often reveals that these drinks contain a high percentage of water, added sugars and artificial flavours, with only a small fraction of fruit juice. This practice misleads consumers into believing they are purchasing a healthier, fruit-based beverage when, in reality, they are consuming a product with high sugar content and artificial additives, contrary to the healthy image presented on the packaging.

Yet another example of such misleading claims is in the real estate industry. Developers may advertise under-construction properties with attractive brochures featuring 'provisional' mock-up apartments with high-end finishes, spacious layouts and amenities like swimming pools, gyms and landscaped gardens. However, the property developer may sell these apartments without necessary approvals for their advertised claims.

Another example of misleading labelling is in financial products like credit cards. Credit cards often offer attractive introductory interest rates that spike dramatically. Similarly, they can charge high fees for balance transfers, late payments or exceeding the credit limit, which the customers are not informed of well in advance, especially when selling the product. The information about the later spike or the extra charges is often written in fine print; hence, these businesses prey on the short attention span of buyers.

These businesses contrast with transparently labelled and described products, such as a bank loan from a respected bank in India, where all the information about the instalments, extra costs and penalties is disclosed, allowing the buyer to make an informed decision.

Raising Barriers to Entry, Not Quality

One more dirty way businesses attempt to maintain their profits is by ensuring the absence of competition, i.e., by deliberately raising barriers to entry into the industry. Such strategies are called rent-seeking strategies. One of the classic examples of such rent-seeking, which ironically gets glorified in strategy courses, is the cola industry, which engages in tactics aimed to lock in bottling companies through peculiar long-term contracts that debar these companies from doing business with their competition while offering them exclusive territorial rights in return. In this way, they debar their competition, especially smaller players, from developing the bottling capacity to sell their products.

The pharmaceutical industry uses the malpractice of 'evergreening' to maintain entry barriers by extending the length of their patents, making minor enhancements to their drugs and extending their monopoly. Patents are a unique system offering temporary monopoly rights over an innovation to the creator. There is a good rationale for patents—innovation, especially in industries like pharmaceuticals, can be costly. Still, once the innovation has been made, it may be easy for competitors to replicate. This creates a problem; if all innovations get imitated, businesses would not be incentivised to innovate.

Another feature of patents, critical for producing social good, is that when receiving these temporary monopoly rights, the innovator must make the details of the innovation public knowledge. This ensures that innovations are not trade secrets. By offering temporary monopoly rights to innovators in return for public disclosure of an innovation, patents ensure that the frontier of knowledge can be advanced while also protecting the interests of the innovator. However, patents can be misused when monopoly rights are extended, even without substantial innovation. Such 'evergreening' policies then create artificial barriers to entry for new players who may drive down the costs of medicines or enhance their effectiveness.

An example of such 'evergreening' is the mental health drug Prozac, developed by Eli Lilly. The company received its patent in 1987, set to expire in 2001. As the expiration date approached, Eli Lilly sought to extend market exclusivity through various tactics. They introduced new formulations and variations of Prozac, such as a weekly version of the drug, which provided a slight modification to the original daily dosage. This allowed them to file for new patents, extending their monopoly on the drug beyond the original patent expiration date.

Another manner in which businesses with deep pockets can raise entry barriers is by offering their products at unsustainably low rates for an extended period to drive out competition. Once the competition exits and the business has developed its monopoly, prices are increased. Amazon is especially noted for such tactics. For example, in the early 2000s, Amazon aggressively priced books and media products below cost to gain market share from traditional bookstores and smaller online competitors. Independent bookstores and smaller chains struggled to match Amazon's prices, leading to the closure of many local stores.

Lately, several start-ups have adopted this 'burning cash' model, underwritten by large venture capitalists and investors. In this model of entrepreneurship, the start-up offers unsustainably low prices as 'promotions' to attract customers, burning cash for extended periods, attempting to drive out others, especially small traditional players, from the competition.

The Amazon Model

Amazon earned almost no profits for the first seventeen years of its business (1997–2014), but its profits soared afterwards.

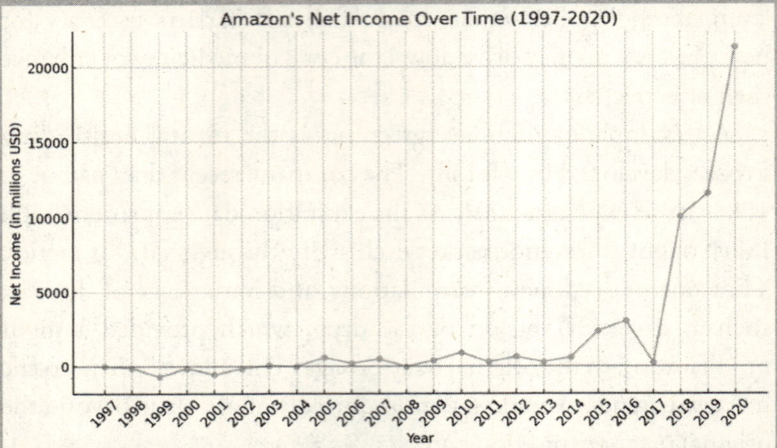

One of the ironies of such start-ups, which was also true for Amazon, is that they enjoy a valuation of above a billion dollars but cannot make a profit. Their high cash burn rates (which drive losses) are presumed to eventually turn them into monopolies, giving them sustainable profits. Amazon is the poster child of this approach.

Another manner in which businesses can increase entry barriers is by levying switching costs from customers when they wish to try out a different business. Businesses do this by bundling their popular services with unpopular ones. Microsoft became a target of regulation in 1998 when it attempted to bundle its internet browser (Internet Explorer) with its dominant operating system (Windows). Microsoft was accused of misusing its monopoly position in one industry (operating system industry) to stifle competition in another (internet browser industry) by bundling its products, which hurt businesses like Netscape Navigator. The US courts in 2000 ruled that Microsoft should be broken up into two companies, but this judgment was overruled. Eventually, in 2001, it was settled that Microsoft would share its application programming interfaces (APIs) with third-party companies to ensure that such companies could develop software compatible with Windows. Such transparency eventually became an industry standard.

The operating system industry is often a space for dirty monopolistic practices. For example, both Google and Apple have been accused of misusing their dominant position in the mobile operating system industry to squeeze profits from small app developers. They charge app developers a significant commission (typically 30 per cent) on sales and in-app purchases made through their app stores. They also require apps to use their in-app payment systems, preventing them from using alternative, potentially cheaper, payment methods. These practices have been controversial. The legal battle between Epic Games and Apple is a notable case that illustrates these issues. In August 2020, Epic Games, the developer of the popular video game Fortnite, introduced a direct payment option in the Fortnite app, allowing players to purchase in-game currency at a discounted rate by bypassing Apple's payment system. This move directly violated Apple's App Store guidelines, which mandate the use of Apple's in-app payment system and the associated 30 per cent commission.

In response, Apple removed Fortnite from the App Store, preventing new downloads and updates for existing installations. Epic Games promptly filed a lawsuit against Apple, accusing the company of monopolistic and anti-competitive practices. Epic argued that Apple's control over the iOS ecosystem and its requirement to use its payment system constituted an unlawful monopoly, stifling competition and innovation and harming consumers and developers. Simultaneously, Google also removed Fortnite from the Google Play Store for a similar violation, leading Epic to file a lawsuit against Google with similar allegations.

The matter is still under judicial and regulatory review. While the US courts found Apple's 30 per cent charge to be non-monopolistic, they found its attempts to stop apps from sending their customers to alternate stores anti-competitive, leading to a partial victory for Epic Games. However, these practices have been taken more seriously in the European Union, which has passed the 2022 Digital Markets Act to regulate monopolistic practices of 'gatekeepers'. Key provisions include requiring gatekeepers to allow alternative payment systems and prohibiting self-preferencing their services.

Name of the organisation/industry	Dirty strategy employed
DuPont	Lobbying and using networks to evade regulatory costs related to pollution (e.g., Teflon poisoning case)
Fossil fuel industry	Lobbying against regulations, promoting climate denialism through think tanks like the Global Climate Coalition

Name of the organisation/industry	Dirty strategy employed
Large internet companies	Lobbying against user privacy regulations, promoting anti-privacy laws (e.g., European Privacy Association backed by companies like Microsoft, Google, Yahoo)
US tobacco industry	Lobbying against smoking hazard warnings and regulations, delaying critical health warnings despite evidence of harm
Food industry	Misleading marketing on product labels (e.g., 'fresh' fruit juices containing high percentages of water, added sugars, and artificial flavours)
Real estate industry	Misleading advertising for under-construction properties, selling without necessary approvals
Financial products (credit cards)	Misleading customers with attractive introductory interest rates that spike later and hidden fees, preying on customers' lack of attention to fine print
Cola industry	Raising barriers to entry by locking in bottling companies with exclusive contracts, preventing them from working with competitors
Pharmaceutical industry	'Evergreening' patents to extend monopoly on drugs (e.g., Eli Lilly's Prozac), blocking competition with minor modifications and new patents

Name of the organisation/industry	Dirty strategy employed
Amazon	Predatory pricing to drive out competition, then raising prices after achieving market dominance
Start-ups with high cash burn rates	Offering unsustainably low prices to drive out traditional competitors, aiming for future monopoly profits despite current losses
Microsoft	Bundling popular services with dominant products (e.g., Internet Explorer with Windows), leveraging OS monopoly to stifle competition in browser market
Google and Apple	Charging high commissions (30 per cent) on app store sales and in-app purchases, mandating use of their payment systems, stifling cheaper alternatives

7

Self-correcting Markets

Markets can correct many dirty strategies.

If businesses conduct so many potential malpractices across industries, should they not be regulated more? This is a fair question. Let us consider the dirty strategies discussed previously and the various challenges in regulating them.

Our first set of dirty strategies involved lobbying, quid pro quo and astroturfing to evade regulatory action for the negative externalities (such as pollution) caused by products like Teflon, fossil fuel, cigarettes and the internet. Regulating lobbying involves regulating the regulator, a classic problem. We may be able to police the crime away, but who will police the police? Moreover, if an apex police officer can police the police, then who will police that apex police officer, and so on? Even if one can create a perfectly policed state, is it worth living in such a society, with the heightened level of surveillance and 'vigilance' at all levels?

In the early 2010s, India entered a period of growth slump. One cause of this slump was considered to be policy paralysis, triggered by fear in the minds of decision-makers (due to an expose of a variety of scams, e.g., 2G, coal, 2010 Commonwealth Games) that their decisions may come under the ambit of scrutiny by higher-ups. Consequently, decision-makers, especially in government, refrained from making any major decisions. This paralysis had several detrimental effects on the economy. Infrastructure and development projects faced significant delays due to the lack of decisive action, impacting growth and development initiatives. The business environment became uncertain, causing a decline in investor confidence as domestic and international investors hesitated to commit capital, fearing regulatory and bureaucratic bottlenecks.

When thinking of regulation, we need to strike a balance. While some external regulation is necessary, such as policies around how businesses should manage their waste, others, like what prices taxi drivers charge their customers, can be controversial. Hence, we should return to the basics and ask if markets can self-regulate.

The Power of Buyers and Suppliers

When businesses pursue dirty strategies and try to squeeze their stakeholders, there are various situations where they get punished by market stakeholders such as customers, suppliers, buyers, employees, competitors or innovative new entrants.

For example, the cola industry has been undergoing a decline once *customers* realised that cola was a cause of obesity. Similarly, the tobacco industry underwent a similar decline, with greater awareness of the ill effects of tobacco. Generally, when businesses offer low quality or levy high prices, they are punished directly by customers, leading to the adage 'Customer is King'.

In the same way, strategies to squeeze *suppliers* can be costly for businesses, too. An example is when music superstar Taylor Swift took her entire music catalogue from Spotify in 2014, concerned by low royalty payments to artists by increasingly monopolising streaming platforms. She wrote, 'Music is art, and art is important and rare. Important, rare things are valuable. Valuable things should be paid for.'[41] The loss of such a dominant artist from their catalogue shook the company and created a debate about musician and producer rights in platform businesses. Taylor Swift eventually returned to the platform in 2017 when Spotify began offering artists better compensation and deals.

Buyers (B2B businesses, retailers, importers) are important market-based regulators pushing producers to adopt quality, labour and environmental standards. A good example of this has been Nike. In the 1990s, Nike faced severe public backlash for poor labour practices in its Asian manufacturing facilities, including low wages, unsafe conditions and child labour. In response, Nike launched a significant transformation by establishing a comprehensive Code of Conduct for its suppliers, mandating fair wages, reasonable working hours and safe conditions and prohibiting child labour. To enforce these standards, Nike implemented regular audits conducted by internal teams and independent third parties and began publishing detailed reports on its progress and factory conditions to enhance transparency. This set a new industry benchmark for corporate responsibility and influenced other brands to adopt similar ethical practices. Other organisations known for raising standards among their suppliers include Apple, Starbucks, Walmart and Unilever. Additionally, as an importer, the European Union requires certain certification requirements for exporters, further driving improvements in global production standards.

The Power of Employees

Employees traditionally have been powerful regulators when businesses try to squeeze their wages and benefits. The history of industrialisation and labour rights, described in earlier chapters, illustrates this. The Tatas have been pioneers in offering favourable employment conditions, making them attractive destinations for employees and workers, allowing them to excel in diverse businesses, from hospitality to steel and car manufacturing to IT consulting.

Conversely, businesses can become completely paralysed if they face severe employee backlash. A recent example is OpenAI, which faced major turmoil in late 2023 when its board abruptly dismissed CEO Sam Altman. This decision led to dissent among the employees, with over 700 staff members signing a letter demanding Altman's reinstatement and threatening to resign if their demands weren't met. The situation escalated as employees expressed their frustration publicly and internally. The intense pressure from the workforce and the potential mass exodus of talent forced the board to reconsider their decision, eventually leading to Altman's return and the resignation of several board members. The situation demonstrated the significant influence employees can exert, showcasing how internal conflicts can lead to dramatic shifts in corporate governance.

The Power of Competition

Competitors themselves can act as major regulators of businesses. A good example is how Apple has addressed privacy concerns in response to practices by companies like Facebook. To position itself as a pro-privacy business, Apple introduced several features in its iOS mobile operating system designed to enhance user privacy and limit app data collection.

In 2020, Apple rolled out the App Tracking Transparency (ATT) feature, which required apps to request user permission before tracking their activity across other companies' apps and websites. This move significantly impacted companies like Facebook, which rely heavily on monitoring user data for targeted advertising. The new privacy feature led to a decline in ad revenues for Facebook and other similar businesses, as users were given more control over their personal information, and many chose to opt out of tracking.

Finally, poor business practices can be regulated by *new innovative entrants*. A good example is the disruption of the traditional taxi industry by Uber and other ride-hailing companies. The taxi industry was traditionally regulated to ensure the safety of riders. These regulations included licensing requirements and vehicle and driver standards to protect passengers and maintain service quality. However, this system led to fewer taxis, driving up consumer fares and poor and unreliable service quality. Taxi associations resisted technological advancements, such as GPS and credit card payments, preferring to maintain the status quo, acting as monopolistic taxi associations in a city.

Uber's entry into the market in 2009, and then of other companies like Ola and Lyft, revolutionised the traditional taxi industry by introducing a convenient, app-based platform that allowed users to quickly hail rides, track their drivers in real-time via GPS and pay seamlessly with credit cards, all through their smartphones. This innovation significantly reduced wait times and improved the overall customer experience. This model also offered more competitive pricing, often undercutting traditional taxi fares by leveraging dynamic pricing based on demand. Additionally, the rating system for drivers and passengers enhanced accountability and service quality, addressing common complaints about driver behaviour and vehicle cleanliness.

The disruption forced the traditional taxi industry to adapt or risk obsolescence, highlighting how new entrants with innovative solutions can effectively regulate and transform established but inefficient industries.

Market Stakeholder	Role in regulating dirty strategies	Example
Customers	Directly impact businesses by changing buying behaviour in response to poor practices	**Cola Industry**: Decline due to increasing awareness of obesity caused by sugary drinks **Tobacco Industry**: Decline with rising awareness of health risks
Suppliers	Can withdraw their goods/services or demand better terms, impacting the business operations	**Taylor Swift and Spotify (2014)**: Swift removed her catalogue from Spotify over low royalty payments, forcing Spotify to improve compensation for artists.
Buyers (B2B, retailers, importers)	Push for better quality, labour, and environmental standards from their suppliers	**Nike (1990s)**: After a backlash for poor labour practices, Nike implemented a Code of Conduct and regular audits, setting new industry standards.
Employees	Can organise protests and strikes or threaten to leave, forcing businesses to reconsider their policies	**OpenAI (2023)**: Employees threatened mass resignation after CEO Sam Altman's dismissal, leading to his reinstatement and board changes.

Market Stakeholder	Role in regulating dirty strategies	Example
Competitors	Drive changes by offering better alternatives or highlighting poor practices of rivals	**Apple and Privacy (2020)**: Apple's App Tracking Transparency feature impacted Facebook's ad revenue by giving users control over data tracking.
New entrants	Disrupt the market by introducing innovative solutions that address inefficiencies or poor practices	**Uber (2009)**: Disrupted the taxi industry by offering convenient, app-based services with better pricing and accountability, forcing traditional taxis to adapt.

8

The Role of Regulators

Some external regulation is indispensable in business even though it can be prone to capture.

THERE is some truth in the notion that perfect markets, where there exists competition between buyers and sellers and little to no information asymmetry in the market, can be self-regulating. To put it differently, *first,* if there are sufficiently powerful market stakeholders who can influence a business, and *second,* any information about dirty strategies employed by a business is promptly available to others, then these market stakeholders can punish those businesses that adopt dirty strategies. However, these conditions are usually not true in real-life scenarios.

A good example of a situation where both conditions failed is DuPont, which was a dominant player in the US chemical industry and held a monopoly over Teflon. Additionally, it was one of the few entities (along with 3M) that had some clue about the ill effects of the C8 chemical used in Teflon, which it actively tried to suppress. The rare and slow nature of the impact of the chemical meant that there was not a large group of people who were visibly affected by Teflon poisoning. Hence, the information about its ill effects did not reach the public for decades. It took several more decades for some action to be taken on the chemical. Hence, the market regulation approach failed.

There is no particular reason to believe that actual markets are autonomously efficient at information revelation or that they are competitive spaces where businesses are at the mercy of market stakeholders. Hence, a few other stakeholders, called non-market stakeholders, become essential for regulating dirty strategies, chiefly among them being civic groups and the media; these non-market stakeholders are crucial, as they are the voice of a variety of stakeholders, including those who may be harmed by a business's externalities (e.g. pollution), without being its direct customers.

Non-market Regulators

Civic groups have often been at the forefront of making society aware when organisations employ dirty strategies. Such groups comprise a variety of entities: local communities, environmental groups, non-government or non-profit organisations (NGOs), think tanks, universities, scientific and professional associations, special interest groups, political parties and more. Labour unions are also part of civic groups, but they are also essential market stakeholders.

In the DuPont case, the key stakeholders who demanded accountability for the business were the informal civic networks, which represented the interests of persons affected by the toxic effects of Teflon. Without their presence, the toxic link between Teflon and various diseases and disabilities could not have been uncovered.

Yet another essential non-market stakeholder, distinct from civic groups, is the media. Media, especially investigative journalists (like the International Consortium of Investigative Journalists, ICIJ), have a critical and distinct role in societies—they are the bearers of information necessary for keeping different stakeholders informed. The newspaper *The Indian Express* played a crucial role in 2018 in exposing a scandal involving a major private Indian bank, ICICI, related to a quid pro quo bank loan to the conglomerate Videocon Group. ICICI Bank sanctioned significant loans to the Videocon Group, which became non-performing assets in 2008. The newspaper disclosed in March 2018 that the chairman of Videocon had invested in a company owned by ICICI Bank CEO's spouse soon after receiving the loan from the bank.[42] This exposé raised serious questions about the bank's impartiality in the loan sanctioning process, prompting corporate, regulatory and legal actions against the bank and the CEO.

An important way media can expose malpractices is through whistleblowers, who openly or discreetly inform the public through journalists about observed malpractices in organisations. A key whistleblower of the ICICI-Videocon case was Arvind Gupta, a shareholder of ICICI Bank,[43] who first wrote about his suspicions about the malpractices in a blog and then as a letter to the prime minister in 2016. However, as a whistleblower, he may not have had all the documentary evidence to support his suspicions, and his concerns were not immediately flagged. In 2018, investigative journalism by *The Indian Express* provided further details about the case, which became a subject of investigation by regulatory bodies.

In the DuPont case, whistleblowers like the Tennant family were the first to raise issues about Teflon's toxic properties. A lawyer (Robert Bilott) picked up the issue (not the media) and eventually brought it to national and regulatory attention through the activism of local community groups.

Social Media as a Regulator

An important thought experiment to consider is how the DuPont case would have played out in the age of social media. Social media would naturally be able to uncover such issues sooner by more quickly lending a voice to victims of Teflon poisoning. In many cases, social media certainly allows diverse voices to have a platform. However, are their voices enough to gain national salience? This question does not have an immediate and obvious answer.

In many cases, social media has helped expose the dirty strategies of businesses. For example, in 2017, US airline major United Airlines followed its controversial practice of overbooking flights and dramatically denied a passenger with a confirmed ticket to board the flight. The issue gained national attention. A video where the passenger, a doctor, was forcefully dragged out of the plane went viral, leading to widespread condemnation and forcing the company to make policy changes. In an era where everyone has a camera, detecting and reporting dirty strategies has become faster and easier. However, in many instances, dirty strategies may not go viral. For example, the poor working conditions of workers in low-income countries producing garments for the fast fashion industry have not gained the visibility they deserve. What makes some issues viral, others not, remains a tricky question.

Formal Regulators

Beyond market and non-market stakeholders, there are formal institutionalised regulatory bodies like the Securities and Exchange Board of India (SEBI) for stock markets and the US Food and Drug Administration (FDA) regulating the food and pharmaceutical industry. While many regulators focus on particular industries, other regulators may have a purview over businesses of the entire economy (e.g., the Competition Commission of India or the US Federal Trade Commission).

Formal regulators are usually interested in the level of competition in a market, and the general welfare businesses create, intervening in their functioning either through set rules (*rules of the game*) or as and when they deem a business or a market poorly self-regulated. Not all industries need formal regulation, but some of them significantly impact the broader society. For example, some may produce 'essential goods', such as the pharmaceutical and telecom industry. Other industries may impact how much they pollute or create negative externalities, such as tobacco and mining. In such cases, having an authority who looks out for the 'public interest' or 'social welfare' and nudges or coerces businesses to move in that direction is usually considered good.

For example, countries worldwide regulate the price and quality of pharmaceutical products, attempting to make them broadly accessible and safe, well-tested for side effects and duly documented and packaged. Telecom regulators may have similar goals of enhancing accessibility and penetration of telecom.

All regulations do not have to be technical about market issues like price and quality. Some regulations are ideological, based on specific interpretations of 'welfare'. For example, should telecom regulators bring rules that increase the privacy of telecom users, which is usually the case in democratic nations, or should they bring regulations that provide government authorities the ability to look into private communications in the name of security, which is true for autocratic and less democratic nations? The US, soon after the 9 September 2001 attacks, enacted the Patriot Act, which gave the government the power to pry into private communications. India, too, tries to follow a balancing act between privacy and surveillance. Countries and political parties can differ where they belong on this spectrum.

Along with the importance of an industry in broader society, the nature of concentration in the industry also influences the intensity of regulation. In highly competitive industries, where entry barriers are low, there may be a limited need for regulation, as competition can drive customer welfare and public interest.

However, in industries where entry barriers are high (such as the telecom industry) due to very high initial capital investments or which are natural monopolies, there may be only a few powerful businesses operating, creating the need for regulation.

Power supply networks are an example. They tend to be regulated not only because they are an essential service but also because the industry is a natural monopoly—two competing businesses cannot offer power supply in the same geography by laying two competing power lines. In such industries, businesses either tend to be publicly owned or, at other times, they tend to be time-bound private monopolies that are highly regulated, with set limits on prices and service quality. Other industries that are natural monopolies include railways, port operations and water supply.

Regulators like the Competition Commission of India and the US Federal Trade Commission usually attempt to motivate competition. Hence, if they observe mergers and acquisitions (M&A) in an industry that can reduce competition, they could prevent them or put specific restrictions in place. Alternatively, if such regulators find that a business has grown into a large monopoly, hampering competition and entry into the market, they also enjoy powers to levy hefty fines or break down the business.

Walmart faced several regulatory hurdles when entering the Indian market. In 2007, Walmart entered India through a joint venture with Bharti Enterprises to operate wholesale stores. However, they faced significant challenges due to India's stringent foreign direct investment (FDI) policies, which did not allow foreign companies to operate in multi-brand retail directly at that time. Widespread concerns and protests about the impact of large foreign retailers on small local businesses further complicated their entry, increasing uncertainty in their business and stalling their plans for full-scale operations.

Walmart eventually entered the Indian multi-brand retail market via e-commerce with the acquisition of India's homegrown e-commerce giant Flipkart in 2018. The CCI approved this acquisition, but concerned about the potential abuse of a dominant market position, it levied specific conditions such as maintaining fair pricing practices, ensuring non-discriminatory treatment of sellers on Flipkart's platform and adhering to sourcing requirements from small and medium-sized enterprises.

The most visible forms of regulation are national regulators like the FDA, SEBI and the CCI, which are public regulators. In the Indian media industry, the Central Board of Film Certification is a public regulator having the power to certify and regulate the movie industry. However, there are other forms of regulators, too, and often, many different types or levels of regulators operate within the same industry at once. In India, several independent and decentralised bodies regulate and set standards for a sensitive industry like the media, which can be prone to censorship and political influence if regulated entirely by a centralised regulator.

Regulators can also be private industry associations (private regulators) such as the News Broadcasters and Digital Standards Authority (NBDSA) in India, which sets guidelines and standards for broadcasters, digital publishers, journalists and news agencies. Despite such public and private regulators, industry standards in the media industry are often regulated through decentralised journalistic norms promoted by organisations like the Press Trust of India and the Editors Guild of India, which represent the interests of newspapers and journalists in the country. These various layers of regulation ensure a diverse and balanced approach to maintaining ethical and professional standards in the Indian media industry.

What kind of non-market and formal regulators should an industry have, if any? There is no one-size-fits-all answer to this question. Some industries, like pharmaceuticals, may need more centralised regulators, while others, like the media, may need more decentralised ones.

Capturing the Regulators Themselves

Can we expect the regulators to be benevolent bodies that consider the public interest? Often, this is not the case. Politicians and regulators can be more interested in their interests than the public's. Even in well-functioning democracies, regulators are prone to *regulatory capture*, where instead of working in the interest of the public, these authorities (or individuals in these authorities) begin to work in the interest of the entities they are meant to regulate. Such capture can be through various methods like bribery of cash or kind, political donations and revolving doors.

The absence of prompt action by the US Environment Protection Agency (EPA) to investigate cases of Teflon poisoning and take corrective action until the mid-2000s is a reminder of regulatory capture. A variety of dirty strategies related to 'managing' externalities that we have discussed about DuPont ('managing' the toxic effects of Teflon), the fossil fuel industry ('managing' climate change science), large internet companies ('managing' regulations on user privacy) and the tobacco industry ('managing' regulations related to tobacco marketing and sale) attempted to influence the regulatory bodies, including regulators, executive, legislators and, in some cases, the judiciary.

Another potent form of capture is the capture of non-market stakeholders like the media and civil society groups. Media capture is an old and perennial issue, where business and political interests may have outsized influence over media bodies through various methods, inhibiting their journalistic independence. First, media can be captured through ownership—many prominent media organisations become owned by individuals or businesses with other business interests. Second, media can also be captured through advertising, where media organisations are unwilling to report on controversial topics related to their major advertisers, fearing loss of ad revenue. Similarly, civic society can be captured through donations and 'astroturf' as fronts of special interest groups in the guise of independent grassroots movements. Academics, too, can be captured in the same way, through sponsored research projects or preferential access to data, with an implicit expectation of positive bias.

Not all activities that could lead to capture may be corruption. For example, political donations, lobbying and hiring ex-regulators in businesses they regulate (revolving doors) are legal. Similarly, businesses regularly donate to NGOs as part of their corporate social responsibility, advertising is intrinsic to the media industry model and private media ownership is normal and even desirable in a democratic society. These activities turn into capture when businesses begin to use these associations, such as donations, advertising, jobs and ownership, as leverage to limit the independence of these organisations.

Capture limits the effectiveness of formal and non-market regulators, and they can be generally perceived as 'bought' by the entities they are supposed to regulate. Capture may be difficult to prove legally, but it is often apparent. For example, the rampant and haphazard construction of apartment complexes in Indian cities, usually bypassing planning and environmental norms, could not have come about without various forms of capture and corruption in the system.

The problem of capture shows how neither market nor non-market, nor formal regulation, is enough to inculcate good behaviour in organisations. Is bad strategy, then, our destiny? Not necessarily.

9

Good Strategies Innovate

Good strategies improve the product and processes and need whole ecosystems.

THE problem of capture showed us the limits of regulation. Markets do not always self-regulate, and external regulators like media, civic society and formal regulatory bodies may not always act independently due to capture, limiting how well dirty strategies and their ill effects can be regulated.

In the end, internal regulation in the form of empowered managers and employees who consider a high standard of conduct part of their job is a must. However, realistically, such high standards of conduct can only be shown by organisations with strong capabilities that can withstand any poor tactics of their competitors. Businesses without strong core capabilities, even with good intentions, are likelier to adopt dirty strategies and shortcuts for success in response to their competition when business becomes a race to the bottom. Hence, it becomes essential for the health of societies and proper conduct in business that organisations have strong internal capabilities that give them distinct and long-term advantages.

As discussed in the first chapter, businesses classically maintain a competitive advantage by offering their products at lower prices than the competition or by offering better features (quality) to charge higher prices or have a greater market share. What underpins such ability to be a cost leader or a differentiator is the ability to innovate, either in the products or processes. Through examples like Toyota and Apple, we explored how the core capabilities of these companies lay in creating social systems that produce consistent process (Toyota) and product (Apple) innovation. Let us now delve more deeply into process and product innovation and what it entails.

The Future of Manufacturing

The Toyota production system showcases a complex social system that underpins a 'lean' and zero-defect system, where individual workers can stop the production line the moment they suspect defects and drive continuous improvement (*kaizen*). Since the 1980s, much has been written about the Toyota production (or Six Sigma and Lean) system and the promise it brings to process innovation. However, the Toyota system is not easy to implement for organisations, as the relational contracts needed for these production systems to work are not easy to replicate.

Following the advances in manufacturing in East Asian countries like Japan, South Korea and Taiwan, China has taken the lead in manufacturing, especially since the 2000s. The mega Foxconn factory cities are a good illustrative example. What makes these plants successful is their ability to produce a variety of highly innovative products (such as the Apple iPhone) on demand and at an unprecedented scale, supported by end-to-end excellence in logistics. Such capabilities did not emerge in a day, and massive investments in infrastructure with the latest technology and monitoring systems were needed. While developed countries had advanced but old infrastructure, China leapfrogged with fresh infrastructure loaded with new technologies that created state-of-the-art logistics systems.

Chinese manufacturers like Foxconn are known to rely on young and skilled workers, who are offered accommodation and food in their factory cities and are regularly trained on set, well-defined processes. The job is high-pressure, and involves long hours (more than a forty-hour work week). Workers usually leave these jobs after working for a few years, unlike in Japan, where a job is considered a lifelong commitment. Hence, the Foxconn model of manufacturing may look similar to Toyota at a distance, but they could not be more different in detail.

As India and many developing countries aspire to be manufacturing hubs in the twenty-first century, which of the two models should their organisations adopt—Toyota or Foxconn? First, both models involve massive investments in infrastructure and logistics, and these capabilities cannot be acquired by individual organisations alone and need support from the government. But beyond public infrastructure, these two models offer stark choices. The Toyota model, although aspirational, is challenging to adopt immediately, as it requires a degree of trust and discipline to develop the relational contracts that Japan has cultivated culturally over a long period. In contrast, the Foxconn model, which runs efficiently but at the expense of worker rights, is unlikely to be sustainable in a country like India, which has a long history of protecting worker rights and has strong media, civil and labour unions, along with a raucous political competition.

Factor	Foxconn	Toyota
Standard work week	Often exceeds 40 hours	Typically 40 hours
Overtime	Significant, often mandatory	Controlled and regulated
Work–life balance	Little to no work–life balance; workers accommodated in 'factory-cities'	Strong emphasis on work–life balance
Employee turnover	High turnover	Low turnover
Average tenure	Months to a few years	Many employees spend entire careers
Temporary workers	Common	Usually permanent workers
Empowerment	Limited involvement in decision-making and improvement	Strong involvement in kaizen and decision-making
Training and development	Targeted training, more focused on meeting production targets	Extensive training and career development opportunities
Safety and conditions	Criticised for poor working conditions	Strong focus on safety and well-being

Interestingly, these two different manufacturing models are being experimented with in India for iPhone manufacturing by Tata Electronics and the Indian subsidiary of Foxconn. Given the worker-friendly history of the Tatas, the new venture Tata Electronics, planning to become a major player in electronics manufacturing in India, is likelier to uphold higher worker standards, and Tata's brand and trust are well placed to create the conditions in which Toyota-type relational contracts can be nurtured within their manufacturing units. In contrast, Foxconn's venture into iPhone manufacturing has already stepped into controversies regarding hiring practices and working conditions, and the company is already adapting to an institutional and cultural environment different from China.[44]

Twenty-first-century manufacturing hence offers two stark choices. The first is embedded in strong worker rights, thus building long-term relationships in a way that the Tatas and the Toyotas have. The second one is a capital-intensive approach that invests heavily in automation and has short-term transactional contracts with workers. The second approach is likely the preferred choice for investors who maximise short-term shareholder profits, as it requires businesses to share less of their earnings with workers (lower labour share). In contrast, the former model of Toyota is embedded in stakeholderism and aimed at long-term, sustainable profits. The latter approach of transactional process innovation will likely face challenges from the media, civil and labour groups and political parties in the long term.

In democratic and open societies, the Toyota approach may be the only way forward. The Foxconn model can only survive in autocratic regimes and flawed democracies in which workers have low incomes, and their protests are suppressed. Hence, they are willing to accept poor working conditions. As supply chains come under greater scrutiny for their labour and environmental standards, the Foxconn model may be even further scrutinised. The higher the number of stakeholders involved in shaping the future of business, the more likely it is that the Toyota / Tata model of stakeholderism will be viable for manufacturing in the long run.

	Autocracies and flawed democracies	**Democracies**
Low-income economy	*Suitable for mass production*	
	Foxconn Model (transaction and high-pressure)	**Toyota Model** (long-term oriented, e.g., the Tatas)
High-income economy	*Suitable for high value production*	
	Toyota Model (for natives) **Foxconn Model** (for less wealthy immigrants)	**Toyota Model**

However, adopting Toyota's culture or building Tata's long-lived trust is easier said than done. It requires a radical reassessment and reimagination of stakeholder relationships based on design thinking principles and grounded leadership to involve and benefit all stakeholders.

The Locus of Innovation

Much like the Toyota Production System, much has been written about innovative organisations and their practices. However, individual businesses (not even Apple) are rarely isolated islands of innovation. Innovation occurs in clusters like Silicon Valley and Boston-Cambridge in the USA, the Golden Triangle in the UK and the rapidly emerging Pearl River Delta in China, which host various organisations: universities, laboratories, businesses and start-ups. Additionally, innovation now also occurs increasingly through various alliances between organisations that may not be geographically proximate to each other.

Where was the locus of innovation in vaccine development during COVID-19? It was not within a single organisation. The race to develop new vaccines showcased the ability of various global innovation clusters/alliances to come together and produce and deploy time-bound innovations.

It involved contributions from several stakeholders, with universities and research institutions being foremost contributors. Famously, the University of Oxford's Jenner Institute was pivotal in creating the widely used AstraZeneca vaccine. The institute's expertise in adenoviral vector technology, developed through prior work on vaccines like Ebola, allowed rapid development and early clinical trials. Similarly, BioNTech, a German biotechnology organisation with close links to the University of Mainz, developed the mRNA technology that became the foundation for the Pfizer-BioNTech vaccine.

The US-based National Institute of Health (NIH) Vaccine Research Centre played a crucial role in developing the Moderna vaccine by conducting early research on the virus's protein structure, which informed the design of the mRNA-based vaccine. In India, the Indian Council of Medical Research (ICMR) National Institute of Virology (NIV) was fundamental in developing the widely used Covaxin vaccine. NIV provided the virus strain and conducted crucial early-stage research that enabled Bharat Biotech, an emerging pharmaceutical major, to develop and test the vaccine effectively.

Beyond universities and laboratories, the involvement of businesses and start-ups was critical in the swift development and deployment of the vaccines. Pharmaceutical major Pfizer partnered with start-up BioNTech, a specialist in mRNA technology, to scale up vaccine development, trials, production and distribution, leveraging its vast resources. Moderna, initially a start-up focused on mRNA therapies, entered into various collaborations, as with Swiss pharma manufacturer Lonza Group, to produce the active ingredient of its vaccine and with US-based Catalent for fill-finish operations.

Another pharmaceutical giant, AstraZeneca, managed large-scale clinical trials and global distribution for the vaccine developed by Oxford. AstraZeneca partnered with the Serum Institute of India (SII), one of the world's largest vaccine manufacturers, and Catalent to produce and distribute the Oxford vaccine. Similarly, Bharat Biotech took the lead role in vaccine development, trials, production and distribution of Covaxin (in partnership with ICMR NIV).

Beyond universities, laboratories and businesses, government support was crucial in the rapid development and distribution of COVID-19 vaccines. Most noteworthy among these was the US government's *Operation Warp Speed,* initiated in mid-2020 at the peak of the pandemic, providing nearly $12 billion in initial research funding, defence logistical support and other government resources to enable accelerated development, production and distribution of vaccines.

The mission-based nature of COVID-19 vaccination might seem like an exceptional response to an extraordinary situation. Still, even in less dramatic circumstances, successful innovation often relies on coordinated efforts from various stakeholders. Consider, for instance, the launch of a new iPhone, a seemingly straightforward consumer product. The rapid and continuous innovation required to bring a new iPhone to market is a monumental task. Apple must constantly monitor technological advancements, materials and manufacturing processes within its supply chains and beyond. These innovations must then be seamlessly integrated into the product, necessitating the coordination of manufacturing at a scale of hundreds of millions of units.

A prime example of this coordination was the introduction of Gorilla Glass in the first iPhone in 2007.[45] Before the iPhone, plastic screens were the norm for mobile phones, but they were prone to scratches and damage. Apple recognised the need for a more durable solution and turned to Corning Incorporated, a glass manufacturing company with a long history of innovation in materials science. Corning had developed a toughened glass called Gorilla Glass, but it was not produced at the scale or quality needed for mass-market consumer electronics.

Apple worked closely with Corning to refine the manufacturing process, ensuring that the glass could be produced in the quantities and quality standards required for a flagship product like the iPhone. Corning scaled up its production capabilities, while Apple integrated the new material into its existing design and production processes.

The iPhone example helps us see why Apple, a company renowned for its product innovation, considered Tim Cook, a supply chain specialist, to succeed Steve Jobs as CEO. Cook's expertise in operations and supply chain management was crucial for navigating the complex web of suppliers, manufacturers and logistical challenges that underpin Apple's ability to innovate and bring new products to market. In the modern world, bringing various supply chain stakeholders together to foster product innovation is a vital leadership skill, making supply chain leaders like Tim Cook suited to guide organisations like Apple.

10

Know Your Village for Creative Destruction

It takes a village to innovate; nurture your village and its risk-takers to embrace creative destruction.

A famous African proverb goes, 'It takes a village to raise a child.' This is true for business and management as well. No single person or stakeholder runs an organisation: it takes a village. It takes a village to innovate and produce a phone or to build a car; a village to produce vaccines, create an EV ecosystem, produce steel or even a single cup of coffee, a soap or a shoe. A dysfunctional village will fail to build any of these things.

In the pre-modern era, it would not be surprising to hold a mindset where villages were seen as personal properties of landlords and their residents as tenants. It would appear strange to somebody from that era to believe that villages and entire countries could be run participatively as democracies, viewing a natural hierarchy as necessary to getting work done.

While the political world in many parts of the world has graduated from such a hierarchical mindset, the world of business and management has still not. The challenges of this century push us to change this by embracing a view where organisations are participative spaces of various stakeholders, each contributing uniquely to its success, with no single stakeholder as its ultimate owner.

The above perspective may seem to contradict the view that investors are the owners of the organisations. It does not. Did the establishment of Jamshedpur and concern for the long-term welfare of employees and communities come at the expense of the shareholder value of the Tatas? No. It turned into an enviable legacy, trust and brand value. Similarly, did a ban on child labour in the early 1900s industrialised nations to enhance working conditions and save children hinder investor interests, who could have turned more profits had their manufacturing used cheap child labour? Not this either. The ban helped children get a better education and secure a better future for themselves and their communities.

Investors and Decision-makers

Should investors alone be the decision-makers in a business? Investors—those who invest capital in a business—are certainly very critical stakeholders in organisations as they take financial risks. The ability to take financial risks is a highly valuable service that investors offer in society, as the future is intrinsically uncertain, and in the absence of such investors, economic growth and entrepreneurship would stall. The fortunes of investors rise and fall with the fortunes of the businesses they invest in. Hence, their trust in an organisation must be rewarded with healthy returns, which is a legal responsibility of the organisation. The organisation cannot and should not take decisions that undermine investors' long-term returns, as it would be a breach of investors' trust.

However, the employees of an organisation are also risk-taking stakeholders and must be recognised as such. Many employees for whom the organisation is the single source of income may get into deep financial and socioeconomic difficulties if they lose their jobs. But increasingly, employees are becoming dispensable and fired unceremoniously without a proper heads-up or notice.

Ironically, we have entered a peculiar phase of shareholderism, where in good times, shareholders reap heavy profits without passing on these benefits proportionately to employees, as observed with falling labour shares in modern economies. However, in downturns, investors cut the losses by pushing the management to fire employees. In such situations, the employees bear the worst risks of the downturn, while the shareholders can even turn fledging businesses into quick profits through layoffs. This scenario was observed in the big tech industry after the COVID-19 pandemic, when hundreds of thousands of employees were fired, and the valuation of the businesses rose with the news. For example, tech giant Meta fired over 21,000 employees post-pandemic and called 2023 its 'year of efficiency'. The CEO of Meta remained at the helm, improving his financial situation even when his strategic decisions led to widespread layoffs. Who owned the risk in the downturn? The investors, the management or the employees?

The culture of unceremonious firing during downturns is deeply problematic. If employees face the downside of risk, they must also have a say in the management of organisations, not necessarily through financial ownership but through proper channels of representation in decision-making. Similarly, local communities also face several business risks by being exposed to pollution and other negative externalities. The DuPont case presents this situation explicitly. If they bear the risks of the businesses, should they not have a say, too?

One of the simplest ways different stakeholders are brought together is through constant engagement and by ingraining design thinking principles and grounded leadership in the organisation's DNA. A more formal and concrete way stakeholders like employees and local communities can be included in the decision-making is by making them a part of the board or by hiring independent directors from such communities. How we compose our boards and the people we pick for our top leadership says a lot about the stakeholders we most value in the organisation.

When organisations fail to care for their village and hear their various stakeholders exposed to its risks, they lose the trust of the public. For example, unceremonious firings in big tech are coming with reputational damage for these businesses among highly skilled job seekers in emerging industries like artificial intelligence (AI), where start-ups with better and less hierarchical management–employee relations are becoming more attractive.

Economic historian Stephen Mihm at the University of Georgia, commenting in Bloomberg on tech layoffs in 2022, said, 'Far from cutting-edge, these layoffs mark a revival of long-discredited corporate strategies. If the trend continues, history suggests these tech leaders will leave their companies severely crippled, at best.'[46] Similarly, researchers Sandra Sucher and Marilyn Morgan Westner, writing in *Harvard Business Review* (2022), found that

> ... companies that conduct layoffs underperform for nearly three years longer (than) those that do not. The reasons are in the well-researched hidden costs of layoffs. Employees who survive the layoff may struggle with anxiety, insecurity, low morale, sadness, and survivor guilt, which lead to disengagement and hinder job performance. Research shows that anxiety about job security, grief for coworkers who were let go, and overwork can reduce innovation. Quality may decline as employees focus on improving

> productivity to keep their jobs. Managing talent becomes more difficult as existing staff resign. Reputational damage may make it harder to attract high-quality new hires.[47]

Fairness is an essential skill for leadership, and organisations that cannot form relational contracts between stakeholders grounded on a sense of fairness and trust will inevitably fail to build the core capabilities needed for innovation and long-term success. Businesses that succeed in developing these relational contracts can raise entire villages (ecosystems) that not just create a thriving business but also bring about creative destruction in their industries, raising themselves to dominant positions. Examples of this are Netflix and Spotify.

Embrace Creative Destruction

All businesses are inevitably disrupted by a more creative innovator—this is the principle of creative destruction. As described by economist Joseph Schumpeter in 1942, creative destruction *is the process through which innovations replace outdated technologies, businesses and industries and has been the ultimate driver of long-term economic growth*. This principle was exhibited well in the music and movie distribution industry, where traditional distribution methods were replaced by new streaming models in the 2000s.

In the late 1990s and the 2000s, the music and the rental video industry lost revenue due to rampant piracy (e.g., through sites like The Pirate Bay). Although a switch to digital content was highly anticipated, key players in this space, like Blockbuster, the dominant movie rental business, or Pandora and Apple iTunes, the early pioneers in digital music, weren't pursuing innovative business models. To make this transition, various activities were required: investing in digital infrastructure, hiring and honing employees in emerging technologies, and entering into long-term licensing deals with a comprehensive roster of movie producers and music labels. Incumbents failed to recognise the scope of activities needed to bring this transition.

The difficulty of making such a paradigm change also meant that the industry stayed stuck in a lull period in which traditional businesses scrambled for a new business model to adapt to the digital age, overshadowed by the threat of piracy. Certain industries, such as newspaper media, still need to recover from the rise of substitutes like blogs and social media, which disrupted their business model, leading to a decline in the newspaper media industry since the 2000s, with no significant alternatives.

The years 2006–07 were watershed in technology. The iPhone was launched, followed by an announcement of the launch of Android. This was also when 3G mobile technology and broadband internet became increasingly common, making the internet faster and helping with the rise of multimedia websites, especially YouTube, which was acquired by Google in 2006 and would be considered the streaming pioneer. Other milestones included the launch of Twitter and the public release of Facebook. Notably, Spotify too was launched in 2006, while Netflix launched its streaming business in 2007, during a time of significant shifts in the digital economy. Unlike Pandora and Blockbuster, Netflix and Spotify were technology companies at their core, and their tech DNA allowed them to attract the talent needed to build large-scale tech streaming businesses that would adapt to and shape these changing trends in the economy.

Initially a DVD rental-by-mail service, Netflix launched its streaming service in 2007, investing heavily in developing content delivery network (CDN) technology to ensure reliable and high-quality streaming. Netflix pioneered the development of recommendation algorithms that attracted top computer scientists with lucrative offers and a highly autonomous work environment, and these technological investments enhanced viewer engagement and satisfaction.

Netflix also secured fair and transparent licensing agreements with major studios and networks, building an extensive content library for streaming on various devices, including smart TVs, smartphones, gaming consoles and computers. Over time, Netflix ventured into original programming with the launch of the popular TV series *House of Cards* in 2013, and very soon, the streaming platform became the platform of choice for many high-profile content producers, creating a name for itself in original programming and boosting its subscription sales.

Spotify engaged in similar ecosystem-building. It was a technology business at its core but with a mission—to convince a sceptical music industry to embrace its streaming business model as the only suitable response to piracy. Previous attempts by companies like Apple and its iTunes music service to make legal music downloads were evolutionary solutions that failed to arrest the decline in revenue in the music industry, as users preferred piracy over paying for music downloads. Instead, Spotify proposed a freemium model, offering free, ad-supported streaming alongside a premium, subscription-based service. It emphasised transparency in royalty payments, providing detailed analytics on streaming data to ensure artists and labels could accurately track their earnings.

These contracting innovations helped Spotify sign licensing deals with various music labels, starting with several small labels and creating an extensive catalogue that is legally and freely available (with advertising). Listeners adapted to streaming, favouring it over the unsafe and illegal practice of piracy. Spotify also invested in technologies and in honing talent, enabling the business to develop personalised and social algorithms, offering a service significantly superior to competing platforms or piracy websites.

The ecosystems developed by Netflix and Spotify brought about paradigm changes in how people consumed media content.

Netflix's on-demand streaming model disrupted traditional television and film distribution. Spotify's success in music streaming changed how music labels saw music, viewing it from the lens of access rather than ownership.

Both these businesses, Netflix and Spotify, were ecosystem builders, investing in technology, human capital and culture needed to build seamlessly personalised streaming technologies at scale. They nurtured a village by supporting various stakeholders, entering into trustworthy and long-term relationships with them during industry uncertainty, creating thriving businesses and redefining the entertainment landscape.

***Pursue ~~profit~~ innovation*:**

- Dirty strategies 'manage' pollution, increase opaqueness and raise barriers to entry to seek rents.
- Markets can correct many dirty strategies.
- However, some external regulation is indispensable in business even though it can be prone to capture.
- Good strategies improve the product and processes and need whole ecosystems.
- It takes a village to innovate; nurture your village and its risk-takers to embrace creative destruction.

Rule 3

HEAR THE ~~TYPICALS~~ ATYPICALS

'Lose money for the firm and I will be understanding; lose a shred of reputation for the firm and I will be ruthless.'

—Warren Buffet, Investor

11

Design Isn't Neutral

Design is not neutral, and who is it designed for is a strategic choice.

We are surrounded by design. From buildings to cities to the tools we use, the clothes we wear, the software we navigate with, design shapes visibly or invisibly how we interact with the world and each other. Good design is often unobtrusive—it does not make itself obvious but sits gently in the background. For example, consider a courtyard that naturally brings people together without them ever consciously realising the effect of the flow of the building on their movement. Similarly, consider paved streets that motivate people to walk, shop, dine and mingle, creating an economy and a community. However, despite the ubiquity of design, designs do not include everyone, and while they can serve some, they can (inadvertently) hamper others. Listening to those who are often forgotten—the atypicals—helps us design better and create better systems and processes.

Design Is Selective

Regardless of what route an urban transit network takes, it is bound to create pockets of inaccessibility for some and centrality for others. How should such pockets be selected, and what principles should they be based on? The choice of principles and the stakeholders we design for will shape the nature of the developed product. Due to the intrinsically subjective nature of design, it may fail to be inclusive. Consider cities with massive multi-lane flyovers that are fantastic for high-speed cars. They are not just unsuitable but also inconvenient for pedestrians, small shops and hawkers. Or, consider the design of nine-to-five traditional workspaces with no space or consideration for employees with childcare responsibilities.

Minor design changes can bring about revolutionary progress in the inclusivity of designs. For example, providing ramps instead of staircases makes spaces much more inclusive for the differently abled and older people. Or a switch from the terms 'spouse', 'husband' and 'wife' to 'partner' as beneficiaries of employment benefits can make workplaces inclusive to queer persons.

Such lack of inclusiveness, even when not deliberate, can lead to major crises. For example, DuPont's top-down organisational design led to an unwillingness to listen to the concerns of its pregnant employees or neighbouring farming communities, causing a major environmental crisis. Similarly, poorly designed health algorithms can have embedded racial biases and raise health costs for patients of certain backgrounds and races. A widely used healthcare algorithm by US developer Optum included healthcare expenses as a proxy for measuring healthcare needs, and it was found in a Harvard study to be systematically biased against Black patients, as it consistently underestimated their healthcare needs because their income was lower.[48]

We need better-designed businesses that are resilient to new information and conscious of their blind spots. However, design is not only not neutral—it is almost always intentional. If a design misses out on considering certain stakeholders, it is either a conscious choice or a result of biased emphasis on just a few.

Design Is Strategic

Design encodes strategy. The iPhone's design encapsulated Apple's strategy. The phone's revolutionary touchscreen, its app-based operating system and the App Store, which is open to third-party developers, enabled Apple to build an ecosystem around its flagship product, allowing it to earn not only from the sale of its phones but also the revenue from the services used over its devices.

Apple purposefully restricted apps from being sold and downloaded in its proprietary market, which was not necessarily the only approach it could have taken. For example, Microsoft Windows followed a more open approach, where software could be bought from anywhere in the form of .exe files and installed on its devices. Google's mobile operating system, Android, also allows users to install apps from other sources. However, Apple's walled-garden approach (which could be viewed as a dirty strategy because it creates entry barriers) allows the company to control the iPhone's entire ecosystem and earn revenue from a variety of channels.

Businesses can intentionally choose to cater to certain audiences. For example, consider social media and the debate over content moderation policies. How much content moderation should Meta do to ensure that hate speech that is usually directed towards particular groups (such as queer people) is censored? Similarly, how much should 'fake' news be regulated on the platform? Twitter, now called X, has reduced content moderation on the platform ever since it was acquired by entrepreneur Elon Musk in 2022.

The difference was apparent from earlier, when COVID-19 and the 2019 US presidential elections led to higher degrees of content moderation for reducing the spread of 'misinformation' and 'hate' on the platform.

Being inclusive can mean good business. A good example is pop star Rihanna's multibillion-dollar make-up business, Fenty Beauty, in collaboration with luxury giant LVMH. Fenty Beauty, focusing on inclusivity, offered its foundation in fifty skin shades, up from the ten or twenty shades offered by traditional beauty businesses. It also brought in models of various ethnicities, races and skin tones to promote its products, pushing other businesses to follow and expand their range. Launched in 2017, the business is nearly $3 billion in size, driven by strong brand loyalty and an image of inclusion.

Despite potential benefits, businesses can be unwilling to make inclusion a part of their strategy when there can be short-term costs and the long-term benefits remain uncertain. DuPont made a calculated decision in 1984 to continue with its Teflon business despite knowing its potential polluting effects. Teflon was a multibillion-dollar business, and had DuPont voluntarily revealed information about its ill effects, it could have potentially come at a significant loss to its revenue and led to job cuts, spiralling the business into a short-term crisis. Although being proactive would have been the right thing to do from an ethical standpoint, given the severity of damages Teflon had inflicted on people, including their employees, DuPont's leadership could not muster the courage to take the challenge head-on, preferring to shove it under the rug, leaving it for some future executive to handle.

The absence of laws in the US that make business executives criminally liable for their decisions that knowingly hamper people's lives helped, too. Even after the whole Teflon scandal came into the public spotlight, it did not bring any significant financial implications for DuPont when compared to the financial benefits,[49] vindicating the cold business decision of the company to sit and do nothing about the Teflon issue. The executives went on to lead comfortable lives.

The various examples show that the design of products and processes includes certain groups and excludes others, and such decisions, whether conscious or unconscious, are nonetheless strategic choices which can have many intended and unintended consequences.

12

Products Have Externalities

Every product designed and sold has externalities, some of which are invisible.

EVERY product comes with an externality, i.e., side effects. Obesity is the externality of sugary foods, and carbon dioxide is the externality of using petroleum as fuel. Industries, too, can create various externalities, and this in turn can put people—often atypical, unheard and less visible—at risk from them.

In *agriculture*, using pesticides and fertilisers leads to water contamination, and the overuse of water from groundwater wells can lead to water depletion, issues currently being faced by farmers in Indian states like Punjab, along with a rising disease load. Global animal agriculture is a major source of methane emissions, contributing to global warming and leading to international calls to embrace a more vegetarian diet.

Another primary industry, *mining*, faces similar or worse issues, with severe land degradation risks, habitat and ecosystem destruction and water pollution. Poor regulation in the industry can give rise to major scandals like the Bellary illegal mining in the 2000s and the presence of mafias conducting illegal sand mining at river beds. Primary industries of *forestry* and *fishing* also pose risks of habitat destruction, with the threat of deforestation, such as the alarming rate of loss of the Amazon rainforest in Brazil and overfishing, exemplified by endangered whale species.

In the energy and power generation industry, the *fossil fuel* industries based on oil, gas and coal directly contribute to carbon emissions. As mining and drilling businesses, they also have additional externalities of land degradation, habitat and ecosystem destruction and water pollution. The British Petroleum 2010 Deepwater Horizon oil spill in the Gulf of Mexico is a prime example. Even the *renewable energy* industry has externalities like disrupting natural land use, habitat destruction and creating chemical (battery usage) and radioactive (nuclear energy) waste.

In manufacturing, major industries like *automobiles*, *aerospace*, *iron and steel* and *large industrial machinery* are major carbon emitters and creators of industrial waste. The *consumer electronics* industry creates e-waste, such as batteries, which are difficult to recycle as they contain toxic chemicals. The short lifecycle of consumer electronic products like smartphones creates large industrial and chemical waste, with poor standards and little regulation to recycle them.

The *food and beverage* industry is a major plastic and water pollution source through food processing and packaging waste. Additionally, the industry may market food and beverages that lead to obesity, diabetes and other health hazards. The *textile and apparel* industry significantly contributes to water pollution through chemical waste, such as the pollution in the Noyyal River near the textile hub Tiruppur, Tamil Nadu.[50] It is also a leading cause of waste, with fast fashion being considered one of the world's biggest polluters.

Few industries are as notorious as the *chemicals* industry for pollution, releasing hazardous chemicals that lead to air, water, and land pollution. Notable cases include the DuPont Teflon case and the 1984 Bhopal Gas Tragedy. The *pharmaceutical* industry faces similar problems with its need to handle chemicals. Both chemical and pharmaceutical products also carry health hazards (toxins and side effects) if their products are not tested well, as seen in the Ranbaxy scandal in the 2000s, where the company was caught faking test results to get US regulatory approval.[51] Similar issues of chemical waste are associated with the *semiconductor* industry.

The construction sector—*commercial and residential real estate* or *public infrastructure* and *utilities*—is a major cause of urban sprawl, leading to habitat destruction, land use disruption and the creation of urban heat islands. These are pressing concerns of urbanisation in developing countries in cities like Bengaluru, India, and Ho Chi Minh City, Vietnam. Additionally, negligence in the quality of utilities can cause severe health hazards to residents. The 2014 Flint water crisis is a good example, where the negligent infusion of lead in water pipes in poorer and majority-Black areas of Flint, Michigan, led to severe health hazards, especially affecting underprivileged children.

The transport sector, with *airlines*, *railroads*, *freight* and *shipping* industries, is a major carbon emitter, a source of air, noise and oceanic pollution. This has led to heightened focus by climate activists on the misuse of wasteful private jets by celebrities and the shipping and import of products that already have affordable local alternatives.

In the services sector, the nature of externalities changes. Industries like *telecom*, *information technology*, and *software* rely on energy-intensive hardware and data centres. For example, AI requires making high-energy computations for every user query, leading to rising concerns about its energy implications and its effects on the environment and climate change. Such computational hardware also produces electronic waste, which would be easier to manage if planned. The telecom industry, relying on electromagnetic radiation, could also create externalities on humans, flora and fauna, which may not yet be fully understood. Additionally, service industries may produce vulnerabilities that lead to data breaches, outages and threats to user privacy, which are major externalities that are not traditionally viewed as pollution. One recent example is the 2024 Microsoft outage that halted entire industries, including the global aviation industry, as many rely on its services.

Data and its handling become crucial in the banking and finance sectors, as in *banking*, *insurance*, *investment* and *asset management*. Fraud and data breaches are major externalities of these industries when the system is poorly designed, with rising cases of digital crimes being salient examples, calling for the need for tighter security. The same is true for the advisory industry, be it *auditing and accounting*, *consulting*, *engineering*, *HR* or *legal* services—misuse of data for personal profit or unethical advice can cause major scandals, such as the role of consulting organisation McKinsey in the US opioid crisis. Additionally, the advisory industry and its exhaustive travel requirements are a source of carbon emissions, which could be reduced. Similar corruption and data misuse issues are major externalities of the *government* sector and its various departments.

In the healthcare sector, significant risks include industries like *hospital and health services*, *biotechnology*, medical and chemical waste and the spread of diseases and infections (contagions). Like other electronics industries, chemicals and e-waste become risks in the associated medical devices industry. The *education* sector may seem relatively innocuous, but it is one of the leading sectors producing paper waste. Additionally, the educational curriculum could induce biases in impressionable minds and be used as a tool for propaganda by those in power, making it one of the most contentious industries for regulation. Much like the education sector, the media sector, which includes *entertainment*, *publishing*, *broadcasting* and *digital media*, can be vectors of propaganda, misinformation and hate against individuals and social groups, all of which are unaccounted externalities.

Various commercial service industries like *food*, *hospitality, personal care* and *retail* are major grounds for waste generation, which is multiple times more per capita than a regular household. The associated *waste management* and *recycling* industry may lead to unintended consequences like shipping waste from developed areas to poorer areas, even though the poor areas are not the producers of such waste, causing evasion of responsibility and health hazards for those who live near these waste dumps.

Finally, the *tourism* industry is a source of major ecological destabilisation, pollution and gentrification, causing a backlash from locals in cities like Barcelona and natural ecological zones like the Himalayas.

Many Externalities Are Invisible

The externalities of a product may not always be known in advance. The externalities of Teflon and the chemical C8 were not widely known to academic scientists, regulators or the public until the 2000s, even when the first suspicions about them arose as early as the 1960s. Similarly, there existed a broad public debate about whether cigarettes caused cancer for decades, with leading statisticians like Ronald Fisher standing in support of cigarette companies in the 1950s. Asbestos, CFCs, DDT and lead are some other chemicals whose toxic ill effects on health have become well-known only over time.

In the same way, the side effects of COVID-19 vaccines, genetically modified foods, 5G and upcoming mobile technologies are hotly debated today. Information about externalities is often revealed as the use of the product expands. For example, plastics were touted as environmentally sustainable substitutes for paper and wood, as using paper and wood led to deforestation. Hence, using plastics was marketed as a sustainable way to save trees. Even though the externalities of plastics were visible in plain sight as non-decomposable waste, it has taken several decades before serious scrutiny of plastic (and microplastic) waste and its ill effects on humans and the environment has begun. In hindsight, the decision to replace paper with plastic was a poor one, motivated by marketing and advocacy from the petrochemical industry.

Carbon emissions are the most salient externalities today across industries. Until the late 1980s, carbon emissions were not considered negative externalities, as the focus was visible or toxic pollution. Greenhouse gases were invisible externalities. As discussed in Chapter 6, vested groups led by organisations such as the Global Climate Coalition (GCC) tried to suppress and delay scientific consensus and public knowledge on the link between carbon emissions and global warming. This only changed in the 2000s, and today, not only is carbon emission accepted as a major form of pollution, but its control and the transition to greener technologies to arrest climate change is considered the single biggest challenge of the twenty-first century.

The externalities of the current digital economy, including its effects on mental health and privacy, are yet another area where there exists little consensus and clarity. Is early exposure to smartphones causing long-term mental 'rewiring' of adolescents, creating an 'anxious generation' facing a mental health crisis, as NYU psychologist Jonathan Haidt suggests in his 2024 book?[52] Have digital giants led us to an age of 'surveillance capitalism', as Harvard academic Shoshana Zuboff claims in her 2018 book, where access to personal data allows businesses to control people's behaviour subtly?[53] Answers to these questions will only become apparent over time.

Several factors delay a faster consensus about the potential side effects of products. We discussed some of these previously: the time it takes to collect enough data to gather irrefutable evidence, the role of vested interests that suppress the relevant data needed for evidence, the dynamics of power that ignore certain voices in favour of others, especially when beneficiaries and the victims are two different groups with asymmetric power.

Another important factor that delays consensus is the difference in ideology about the very definition of externalities and harm. Consider social media and the debate around misinformation, disinformation and hate speech. Is hate speech an externality that should be moderated, and if so, what is its definition? Are religious criticism and blasphemy offensive to users, a form of hate or a fundamental right to speech? What about opinions that are racist, casteist, homophobic or sexist? Is the ability to spread unsubstantiated theories about the origins of the COVID-19 pandemic and the side effects of vaccination a form of mis- or disinformation, or is it free speech? Moderating such content could be seen in two ways: as a form of necessary regulation needed to reduce externalities of hate and false information on the internet, or as an act of censorship of free thought and speech. The two groups would fundamentally differ in how they view any acts of information regulation. Hence, hate speech and fake news represent not just a form of hidden externality but also a subjective externality whose definition differs from one individual or social group to another.

Given how ubiquitous externalities are to any industry and how they can often be not just hidden but also subjective, managers must crucially understand the externalities they may potentially create. Hence, listening to an exhaustive set of stakeholders can help uncover potential externalities that may not have been emphasised earlier. It is better for managers and their business and reputation to proactively and participatively learn about potential externalities and resolve them early instead of reacting once these become unmitigable. We have discussed various techniques that can help us uncover externalities—*strategic design thinking*, *the leadership mindset* and *knowing the village*—assisting managers in learning about externalities sooner and engaging with them innovatively and from the ground.

Design Thinking

When design thinking is used to immerse oneself in the world of various diverse stakeholders, it enables organisations to learn about their issues and asks sooner. However, the method can be less effective if design thinking only focuses on a few typical stakeholders and ignores the atypicals.

Grounded Leadership

The grounded leadership mindset takes this step further by empowering all employees on the ground to be proactive problem-solvers rather than passive instruction followers. The more engaged the employees of an organisation, the more often they come across stakeholders and their concerns.

Ecosystem Approach

Finally, an ecosystem (village) centric approach to business that recognises the centrality of stakeholders in building innovative products and processes ensures that diverse stakeholders are consistently spoken to and heard for feedback, ensuring any issues get detected early.

Industry	Externality	Atypical stakeholder
Agriculture	Water contamination and depletion, health hazards, methane emissions	Cancer patients in local communities

Industry	Externality	Atypical stakeholder
Mining	Land degradation, habitat destruction, water pollution	Indigenous and tribal communities
Forestry and fishing	Habitat destruction, deforestation, overfishing	Traditional fishing communities, human trafficking victims
Fossil fuel	Carbon emissions, land degradation, habitat destruction, water pollution	Communities experiencing extreme climatic events
Renewable energy	Land use disruption, habitat destruction, chemical and radioactive waste	Pastoral communities affected by land conversion
Manufacturing (automobiles, aerospace, iron and steel, large machinery)	Carbon emissions, industrial waste	Poor communities living near industrial zones
Consumer electronics	E-waste, industrial waste	Low-income communities living near dumping sites
Food and beverage	Plastic and water pollution, packaging waste, obesity and health hazard	Poor communities living near dumping sites and contaminated water bodies

Industry	Externality	Atypical stakeholder
Textile and apparel	Water pollution, chemical waste, landfills	Poor communities living near dumping sites and contaminated water bodies
Chemicals	Air, water and land pollution, health hazards	Residents affected by industrial disasters
Pharmaceuticals	Chemical waste, health hazards	Poor and vulnerable families susceptible to predatory practices
Semiconductors	Chemical waste	Communities and workers exposed to toxic waste
Construction (commercial, residential, infrastructure, utility)	Urban sprawl, habitat destruction, land use disruption, urban heat islands, health hazards	Poor communities living in urban heat islands
Transport (airlines, railroads, freight, shipping)	Carbon emissions, air, noise and oceanic pollution	Poor communities living near noisy and polluted hubs
Technology services (telecom, information technology, software)	Energy-intensive hardware, electronic waste, data breaches, outage	Elderly and less technologically literate individuals targeted by online scams

Industry	Externality	Atypical stakeholder
Banking and finance (banking, insurance, investment and asset management)	Fraud, data breaches	Vulnerable individuals becoming victims of fraud; private citizen data being leaked to scamsters
Advisory services (auditing, consulting, engineering, HR, legal)	Data misuse, unethical advice, carbon emissions	Poor communities whose voices were not considered in the consulting process
Government	Corruption, data misuse	Vulnerable groups facing bureaucratic harassment
Healthcare (hospitals, biotechnology, medical devices)	Medical and chemical waste, disease spread, electronic waste	Poor patients exploited by predatory health providers
Education	Paper waste, propaganda	Poor families becoming victims of predatory education providers
Media (entertainment, publishing, broadcasting, digital media)	Propaganda, misinformation, hate speech	Minority and marginalised groups targeted by online harassment and misinformation

Industry	Externality	Atypical stakeholder
Commercial services (food, hospitality, personal care, retail)	Waste generation	Poor communities living near dumping sites and contaminated water bodies
Waste management and recycling	Health hazards from waste dumping	Waste workers and poor communities living near dumping sites and contaminated water bodies
Tourism	Ecological destabilisation, pollution, gentrification	Remote and indigenous communities experiencing ecological harm and cultural disruption

13

Atypical Stakeholders Know First

Atypical minorities help identify externalities and make organisations scientific and robust.

IF we wish to study the externalities of chemical-intensive agriculture, we can visit Malwa, Punjab, which used to be called the 'cotton belt' but today has grown infamous for being the 'cancer belt' of India,[54] as a rising number of cancer patients have contracted the disease in all likelihood due to exposure to carcinogen chemicals in pesticides, which is extensively used in cotton production in the region, and has contaminated much of the land and water. Many of these pesticides are banned in wealthy nations such as Europe due to their high toxicity levels but continue to be used in India, due to apathy towards its rural one-off victims.

Atypicals and Impact

In the mining and forestry industry, the first group of people affected by land degradation and habitat destruction are local communities, often those from *forest-dwelling communities.* This leads to these groups resisting, especially if such mining operations are performed without their consent. Frictions between mining businesses (including the Tatas) and local tribal communities have marred Indian states like Chhattisgarh, Jharkhand and Odisha, where conflict has even turned violent when either group (businesses in conjunction with the State; tribals in conjunction with underground guerilla insurgents) uses armed resistance.

The fishing industry, especially in the deep sea, has many risks. *Workers* in the industry can be victims of human trafficking, being forced to work in difficult conditions without their explicit consent due to one or the other form of coercion, as a report by Human Rights Watch from Thailand suggests.[55] Additionally, as Amnesty International reports, overfishing by ships in international waters also threatens the livelihood of *traditional fishing communities*, for example, on the west coast of Africa.[56]

The fossil fuel industry has already begun to affect *communities facing extreme climatic events in the Global South's coastal and other low-lying regions* through carbon emissions and global warming. These communities have very low carbon footprints but face the consequences of the lifestyle choices of rich people in other nations. Additionally, accidents like the Deepwater Horizon oil spill lead to permanent damage to ecosystems, which take decades to recover, if at all, destroying coastal livelihoods.

Several renewable energy projects, be they in hydel, solar, or nuclear power, face resistance from locals. India has a long history of *local communities* opposing the construction of dams for hydel water projects (e.g., the Narmada Bachao Andolan), which submerge entire communities. Similarly, there has been a rise in protests by *locals* in the Ladakh region[57] about converting local grazing lands into solar power fields, disrupting the local ecology and livelihood.

The manufacturing sector is a source of significant pollution of all kinds, and *people who live near the industrial areas* are the first to report a poor quality of life. It is often the poor who settle in closer proximity to industrial areas like the Okhla industrial area of New Delhi. Environmental regulation was one of the key reasons American and European businesses shifted their manufacturing bases abroad, especially in developing countries with poorer environmental regulations, making manufacturing more affordable, even if unsafe for the local communities.

A deadly example of such a double standard was the 1984 Bhopal Gas Disaster. A chemical plant in Bhopal owned by erstwhile US chemical manufacturer Union Carbide produced hazardous pesticides unsuitable for production in developed countries and followed poor safety, training and maintenance standards. This negligence led to a deadly leak of toxic methyl isocyanate on the night of 2 December 1984, spreading across the densely populated neighbourhoods and immediately killing 3,000–8,000 people, and causing nearly 20,000 deaths in the long run. The number of people facing major or minor long-term health conditions due to the leak is difficult to ascertain and is disputed, and could easily be in hundreds of thousands. The area around the plant continues to be hazardous to date. After the incident, Union Carbide divested its stake in the Indian division. In 2001, Dow Chemical acquired Union Carbide. In 2017, Dow Chemical merged with DuPont. A match made in hell, one might say.

Industries like food and beverage and textile produce a lot of urban waste, often ending up in landfills, and their ill effects of plastic, water and land pollution are first experienced by *people living in slums*, who often live in the 'dirty' and low-lying areas of a city. Otherwise, such slums are built around transport corridors, which are too noisy for more affluent people to live in. Such polluted and unsanitary living conditions expose people to a variety of health risks. Children are especially affected by conditions that impair their full physical and mental development.

The risks embedded in the services industry will likely affect certain groups first. For example, *older people* who are less technologically literate are often likely to be victims of online scams. *Vulnerable people who need money* are at risk of becoming victims of online frauds that make attractive promises of easy money. On social media, *minority groups, like queer people*, are more likely to be the first targets of hate and harassment by online trolls. A 2024 suicide by a queer teenage make-up artist from Ujjain, Madhya Pradesh, due to online harassment on the social media platform Instagram serves as a tragic example.[58] How often are service and advisory providers likely to consider such groups when offering solutions to their clients?

Poor and vulnerable families are more likely to be the victims of predatory medical practices. Such groups more likely cannot afford reputable healthcare options and hence fall for cheaper hospitals that engage in predatory behaviour. Lack of health literacy or the absence of a knowledgeable health worker in the family limits their ability to make informed decisions, making it difficult for them to distinguish good from poor health providers. Lack of insurance coverage and delayed medical attention can also make them susceptible to higher medical charges. Poor and vulnerable families can face similar issues in the education sector.

In the case of tourism, *remote communities* are more likely to report instances of ecological harm (e.g., plastic pollution), as they are most sensitive to sudden increases in tourist inflow and are most likely to advocate for sustainable tourism practices. Tourist agents in bigger, more commercialised cities will likely not have such considerations.

Embrace Scientific Rigour with Atypical Testing

Patients, local and indigenous communities, workers and residents living in polluted areas, victims of environmental disasters, socially vulnerable groups such as queer people, economically disadvantaged families and remote and rural communities—a range of atypical and marginalised stakeholders—are the first victims of the negative externalities of businesses. They are the first to know and raise the alarm, and their concerns need to be central to any decision-making, especially in the modern world. However, such stakeholders are seldom a part of decision-making, but we cannot escape their voices.

Often, managers get into a salesperson mode when promoting their business. Marketing and telling a story that brings forth the product's best qualities in a crowded market are important. However, businesses cannot be run merely by salespersons, at least not responsible businesses that care about their impact on the world. Running a responsible business requires people to adopt scientific thinking.

How is scientific thinking different from salesperson thinking? A salesperson is an advocate who tries to convince others about the best qualities of their product or service. A good salesperson defends when the business is attacked by its critics, trying to tell the best story and give the best defence, which would convince others about how good their product is. They try to manage bad and atypical 'narratives' and attempt to show their products in the best light.

The scientific method approaches problems in a diametrically opposite manner. *A scientist is not a salesperson of their ideas. Instead, the scientist's job is to be the worst critic of their ideas*, willing to listen to as many criticisms as possible of the hypotheses they develop, ensuring that they withstand scrutiny. They attack, not defend their ideas and put them through various robustness tests. They do not advocate for their ideas—they test them until they become robust enough to be out there in the world.

The world would be much better, and businesses would be far more resilient if managers embraced such a scientific approach to doing business. In a 2019 empirical study,[59] SDA Bocconi scholars found that entrepreneurs who embraced scientific rigour performed better, as they pivoted to new ideas sooner when their hypotheses were corrected.

Who is better to test products than atypical and marginalised stakeholders, often the first victims of product externalities? Hence, including atypical stakeholders at the centre of scientific thinking makes complete sense. However, despite its obviousness, this is a rare practice. Testing takes time and diligence, and dirty strategies often gravitate towards salespersonship rather than scientific rigour.

Scientific management has been at the heart of management thinking since the early 1900s. Historically, this term has meant managerial ways to optimise output, forming the foundation of operations management and industrial engineering. At its inception, management was focused on utilising machines and managing labour optimality through time and motion studies. But, over the years, the field became more people-centric, businesses became less about machines and more about people, and workers and other stakeholders began to assert their voices. Human relations and organisational behaviour became significant topics of study, and so did strategy and marketing, which were at the core of how various resources and people can be managed. Through the process of humanisation, management has become less scientific and more driven by theories and frameworks taken at face value as tools for guiding strategy.

There has been a resurgence in scientifically grounded management centred around the spirit of experimentation and hypothesis testing. With the digitisation of the economy, A/B testing has become a common practice. Businesses frequently rely on experiments to determine the efficacy of various strategic, product and marketing decisions. In this approach, two alternative methods are randomly tested with users. For instance, one group of users might receive movie recommendations generated by algorithm A, while another group receives recommendations from algorithm

B. The algorithm demonstrating superior performance with the test groups is then implemented for the entire user base. This method allows companies to make data-driven decisions, ensuring that the most effective strategies are adopted. Businesses have been increasingly adopting such experimentation in making decisions, streamlining speculative decision-making. Mark Zuckerberg, the co-founder of Meta, described this new style of experimental management succinctly, saying, 'Move fast and break things.'[60]

Contemporary scientific management is not only about expanding a culture of experimentation to move fast but also about embracing scientific rigour to proactively detect and address externalities. *Move fast and embrace scrutiny*. By involving a diverse range of atypical and marginalised stakeholders—such as patients, local and indigenous communities, workers in polluted areas and socially vulnerable groups—to robustly and iteratively test their products and processes, organisations can gain early insights into the unintended consequences of their business through such atypical testing. This proactive approach ensures that potential issues are identified and addressed before they escalate, leading to more resilient and sustainable business practices.

Aspect	Atypical testing	A/B testing	Traditional management method
Objective	To proactively detect and address potential negative impacts on marginalised groups	To make data-driven decisions by identifying the more effective option	To optimise resource utilisation and achieve business goals

Aspect	Atypical testing	A/B testing	Traditional management method
Method	Robust and iterative scrutiny of the product and processes from a diverse set of stakeholders	Randomised experimentation with two groups to compare outcomes	Implementation of established management practices, often based on historical data
Stakeholders	Marginalised and atypical stakeholders such as patients, indigenous communities, workers in polluted areas	Customers or users divided into two groups for testing purposes	Internal stakeholders, employees, management, sometimes customers
Time frame	Long-term, proactive identification of issues	Short- to medium-term, focused on immediate results	Varies, often medium- to long-term
Response to criticism	Embrace and address criticism to improve products and practices	Select the option with better performance metrics	Defend existing practices, manage narratives

Aspect	Atypical testing	A/B testing	Traditional management method
Example	Involving local communities in environmental impact assessments, consulting vulnerable groups for product development	Testing different versions of a website's landing page, comparing marketing strategies	Time and motion studies, hierarchical management structures, strategic planning based on past performance

14

Moral and Amoral Drift

Ignoring externalities increases public scrutiny, while ignoring the core product creates the risk of takeover.

WHAT would make managers care about stakeholders and a long list of externalities? Is it a sense of ethics? Let's face it: ethics can be in short supply in a world where greed and short-termism can tempt businesses to adopt less-than-ideal ways to grow. How much will managers who barely manage to produce honest products for their customers care about their externalities on atypical customers? In a world where even customer needs get ignored, is it realistic to believe that the needs of atypical and marginalised stakeholders will be heard?

Non-market Stakeholders Lead to 'Moral' Drift

More than a sense of ethics is needed to push managers to be responsible. In the previous chapters, we have already discussed the power of non-market stakeholders in regulating dirty strategies. Such non-market stakeholders can be said to drift businesses in a 'moral' direction. The term 'moral' here does not imply an absolute sense of morality but a relative one, i.e., pushing businesses in a direction that appears moral to them.

The stakeholder space can be competitive, where different stakeholders are vying for attention and influence. These stakeholders can have varying and often opposing agendas, and they may not take the organisation in a single direction. For example, consider a mining company that is being lobbied simultaneously by two sets of locals. The first wants the business to be built in a certain location as it would create jobs, while the second does not want the business to be located there as it would cause environmental degradation. Hence, the stakeholder space can be a politicised and polarised one.

Few businesses have faced as much public stakeholder scrutiny as social media platform Twitter during the COVID-19 pandemic. During the pandemic, public health organisations and community health advocates wanted strict content moderation to prevent the spread of misinformation that could endanger public health. They advocated for the rapid removal of false claims about the virus, unverified treatments and conspiracy theories, arguing that such misinformation could undermine efforts to control the pandemic. On the other side, free speech advocates worried that there was a risk of overreach that could suppress legitimate debate and diverse perspectives. They also demanded transparency in moderation decisions.

The clash of priorities created a challenging environment for Twitter. Twitter, during this period, engaged in exhaustive content moderation. In the process, its employee count also expanded significantly, from around 4,900 employees pre-pandemic (in 2019) to 7,500 (by 2021), many of whom were involved in navigating the complexities of content moderation. During this time, the market capitalisation of Twitter also rallied from around $20–25 billion (in early 2020) to touch $50 billion (in late 2021), primarily because of the optimism that Twitter had become the essential public square of the world for receiving critical updates. However, in late 2021 and further, Twitter's valuation diminished as it failed to convert the market optimism into substantial user or revenue growth. So, while Twitter's expenses had skyrocketed due to a burgeoning employee count, its revenues did not, spooking the market and erasing its valuation by 50 per cent ($25 billion) in March 2022.

Hostile Takeovers Can Cause 'Amoral' Drift

The drop in Twitter's valuation made it vulnerable and thus a target of a hostile takeover by multi-billionaire Elon Musk, who bought the company at a market premium of $44 billion, vowing to make it leaner and turn it into a 'free speech' platform. After the takeover, Musk immediately fired nearly 50 per cent of the entire Twitter workforce, cutting down on content moderation, much to the ire of stakeholders concerned about hate speech targeted against groups like trans, Black and Jewish people.[61]

Businesses that try to become 'too good' and focus on just mitigating externalities and placating their non-market stakeholders, such that they ignore the expectations of their existing and potential shareholders, become targets of hostile takeovers. Let us understand this important mechanism. Businesses leverage the capital vested in them by investors. Managers (CEOs), who are hired by the board of a business (which represents the owners), have a fiduciary responsibility towards their investors (shareholders) who trust their money with them. Due to this, shareholder interests are considered to be of the highest importance.

Shareholder-value-maximisation may not be a bad principle to follow in a market in which the negative externalities of a business can be either accounted back to the business, if the government resolves those externalities through tools like taxation or subsidies (e.g., carbon credits), or if there are no externalities at all (which is rarely the case). In such a (fictional) world, where the negative costs of a business are accounted for, the surplus value generated by a business is the same as its profit. However, suppose businesses have externalities that are not accounted for or are unresolved by some regulation. In that case, the surplus social value the business generates (including the externality) differs from its profits. In such scenarios, shareholder value maximisation may also create unaccountable negative externalities for society, for which nobody takes responsibility.

Suppose a business like Twitter comprises shareholders that care about the unaccounted social costs (externalities) it produces. Hence, they pursue 'clean' strategies that have lower profits than following 'dirty' strategies. Can such a 'clean' business sustain itself if the social costs are large and all existing shareholders are prosocial, i.e., care about social impact?

In a seminal 2017 paper, economists Oliver Hart and Luigi Zingales argued that it may not, as such a 'clean' business with prosocial shareholders can still become the target of hostile takeovers, where a 'dirty' buyer acquires the business for a value higher than the 'clean' profits the business makes, and then pursue 'dirty' strategies to make a higher net profit.[62]

Individual shareholders, even those who are highly prosocial, will have no incentive not to sell their shares to this 'dirty' buyer, as whether or not the buyer's bid is successful, the individual shareholder is too small an agent to change the outcome of the bid. So, they instead sell their shares to this 'dirty' buyer and make a profit themselves. Only if this collective action problem is resolved by a large number of existing 'clean' shareholders of the business rejecting the takeover (e.g., via a voting system that currently does not exist) can such 'dirty' takeovers be resisted.

Due to the above collective action problem, 'clean' businesses have a risk of 'amoral drift' due to hostile takeovers from 'dirty' buyers who are only interested in maximising profit and will, hence, push the business from 'clean' to 'dirty' strategies. The converse situation, where 'dirty' businesses face hostile takeovers by 'clean' buyers, is not feasible as no private buyer will make an investment that causes a loss to them, assuming that profits brought from 'clean' strategies are lower than 'dirty' strategies. Note that if 'clean' strategies get higher profits than 'dirty' strategies, then no ethical or financial dilemma exists, as no rational investor will pursue the 'dirty' strategy in the first place.

Given the problem of 'amoral drift', managers face dual challenges. If they pursue financially less viable 'clean' strategies, they face threats of potential hostile takeovers. If they pursue 'dirty' strategies, then they face what we can call a 'moral drift' from non-market entities like civil, social and environmental groups, media, academics, politicians, and regulators who would target the business for its various externalities. Balancing these dual threats is not easy. *Ideally, crafting strategies that are both 'clean' and financially viable is the only long-term resolution to these threats. This is where the art and science of strategic stewardship become relevant.*

The Manager's Dilemma

A manager is influenced and shaped by various stakeholders and has to manage both the product(s) and the externalities.

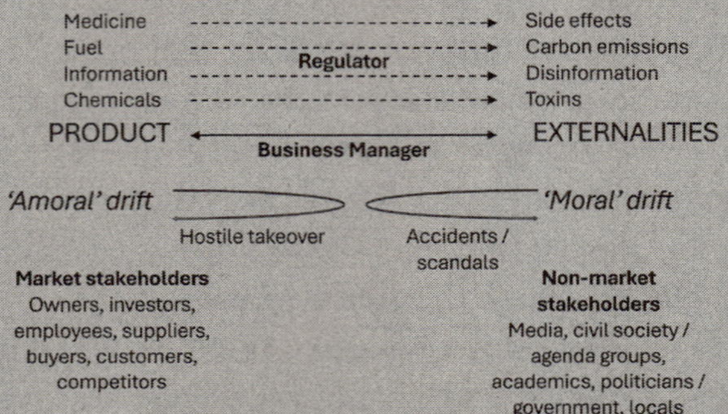

Lessons on Moral and Amoral Drift from Twitter/X

Elon Musk's hostile takeover of Twitter in mid-2022 and the subsequent firing of 80 per cent of staff, including the top management, was highly controversial. Opinions were highly divided over the wisdom of such a move. From a simple operational sense, people like Musk justified such mass layoffs to ensure the company's financial survival, as the business was bleeding money due to its ballooning employee count. However, for the critics of the business, including its past management leaders, such a move came at the expense of eliminating many essential services related to content moderation needed to run a social media platform of the size of Twitter. Who was correct? The answer is complicated.

Now rebranded as an AI-focused business and called X, Twitter is up and running despite its dramatically reduced workforce. New features and additional services have been introduced, such as the AI chatbot Grok, a job service called X Hiring, Community Notes content moderation feature, as well as a subscription service, X Premium. There have been no major outages or operational issues since some early glitches. However, X has struggled to keep its advertisers, many of whom have left the business over concerns about the rising levels of hate speech on the platform. Reports suggest that ad revenue dropped by around 55 per cent in the subsequent year.[63] X tried to pivot towards subscription revenue, but that has not compensated for the loss in advertising income.

X's attempt to attract users with a revenue-sharing model has also not gained much traction. While Musk has claimed that the platform was seeing record user growth, independent analysis has suggested that in February 2024, X had 27 million daily active users on its mobile app in the US, down 18 per cent from a year earlier, and 174 million daily active users worldwide, down 15 per cent from the previous year.[64]

With concerns about continued revenue and user growth, the valuation of X (now privately held) has been estimated to go down from the original $44 billion price Musk paid in 2022 to around $9.4 billion in late 2024, creating a loss of $34.6 billion for Musk.[65]

The challenges faced by X with Musk at the helm have puzzled many, given the legendary image of Musk as an entrepreneur building innovative tech businesses like Tesla and SpaceX and being at the inception of AI major OpenAI. What could be the reasons behind the less-than-impressive results of a business like Twitter under his leadership?

A SpaceX rocket or a Tesla car is an engineering product with clear specifications and requirements. Either can be vertically integrated, and each step of the engineering and manufacturing process could be closely controlled with a 'nanomanager' style of leadership that Musk calls himself. However, Twitter/X is a social product.[66]

Social products are much more difficult to pin down and engineer, as no objective specifications and requirements exist. The requirements and specifications of a social product evolve continually, and both external and internal stakeholders influence not only the demand and supply of the product but also its nature. In companies with a large social component, a more grounded, diffused and participative approach to leadership becomes all the more important. Employees may have a greater need to feel a sense of security in their jobs to do them well, as the objectives and goals of the organisation cannot be as clearly defined as in engineering companies like SpaceX. Social products are unlikely to be successful when nanomanaged, and this could be one of the issues being faced by X.

Pivoting X from a social product to an engineering AI product, as Musk intends to do, may be the best bet for X, given Musk's strengths as a technology nanomanager. For those who wish to build social products, listening to stakeholders is important.

15

Embracing Atypical Testing

Mapping stakeholders, externalities and influence helps in robust atypical testing of organisations.

ORGANISATIONS are no longer isolated units but are increasingly interconnected with society. Many kinds of stakeholders have a voice today in the era of social media, in which brands can be built and destroyed if they ignore or displease certain stakeholders. Of course, this does not imply that all stakeholders have a voice. For example, refugees, displaced, indigenous and extremely poor people have little voice, possibly because they have limited access to the internet to make themselves heard. Additionally, governments use tactics such as internet shutdowns and censorship to limit access to the internet and free digital spaces so that very marginalised groups (e.g., the Uyghur people in China) do not get a voice. Organisations that do not engage with such stakeholders and may have worked in ways to adversely affect the lives of such groups may find themselves in the eye of a storm when their voices gain visibility and prominence one day.

Organisations need to be proactive so that their work positively impacts the world and is (in an instrumentalist sense) robust when facing non-market risks. As we have discussed, atypical testing is a novel way to test one's organisation—both products and processes—for robustness. Atypical testing, at its core, is an essential outcome of the strategic design thinking process that we discussed in the introduction. If strategic design thinking processes do not focus on atypical testing, they fail to do the intended job. Here are some steps that become important when conducting atypical testing.

Make an Exhaustively Diverse and Critical Guest List

We can think of atypical testing as an open house, to which we have invited many people to try our product, test our organisation and examine our processes. Who shall we invite to this testing? Ideally, it is best to invite as many people as possible, but practically, for a deep analysis, there can only be a limited number of people—five, ten, twenty, hundred? The bigger the stakes, the more the invitees. Who should you include in this limited guest list?

With the intended goal of doing atypical testing, this list would include typical stakeholders (e.g., the 'standard' user), as well as those atypical or marginalised. Hence, ensuring that the guest list is as diverse as possible helps capture a wide range of perspectives and potential externalities. This diversity should encompass not only demographic characteristics but also different experiences, expertise and perspectives. Demographic diversity includes age, gender, ethnicity and socioeconomic status, while experiential diversity involves engaging with people with firsthand experience of the issues. Expertise diversity ensures that subject matter experts and advocacy groups with specialised knowledge are part of the conversation. By ensuring exhaustive diversity, businesses can uncover hidden externalities and comprehensively understand their impact, leading to more inclusive and sustainable designs.

An essential principle of atypical testing is to get critical feedback; hence, the organiser should also be willing to do the uncomfortable—inviting critics. Turn your critics into an opportunity to improve your business. Nike successfully did so in the 1990s (as discussed in Chapter 7), when it turned the criticism of poor labour practices in its outsourced factories into an opportunity to create labour, environmental and quality codes for its suppliers.

Legendary investor Warren Buffet showcased a compelling example of inviting critics to the table. In 1991, Salomon Brothers, an investment bank with Buffet's company Berkshire Hathaway as the largest shareholder, was caught in treasury fraud. In the middle of this crisis, Warren Buffet assumed the CEO position. He gave an opening statement to the US Congress when called for questioning about the case, welcoming the investigation and presenting this as an opportunity for Salomon to become a leader in the financial services industry in controls and compliance procedures. His statement is now considered legendary, an example of how businesses should handle and communicate during crises.

Buffet's 1991 Testimony on Salomon Brothers

'I would like to start by apologizing for the acts that have brought us here ... The past actions of Salomon are presently causing our 8,000 employees and their families to bear a stain. Virtually all of these employees are hard-working, able and honest. I want to find out exactly what happened in the past so that this stain is borne by the guilty few and removed from the innocent. To help do this, I promise ... Salomon's wholehearted cooperation with all authorities. These authorities have the power of subpoena, the ability to immunize witnesses and the power to prosecute for perjury. Our internal investigation has not had these tools. We welcome their use ... I also have asked every Salomon employee to be his or her own compliance officer. After they first obey all rules, I then want employees to ask themselves whether they are willing to have any contemplated act appear the next day on the front page of their local paper to be read by their spouses, children and friends...If they follow this test, they need not fear my other message to them: Lose money for the firm and I will be understanding; lose a shred of reputation for the firm and I will be ruthless. I welcome your questions.'[67]

Identify the Externalities They Face and Their Influence

In his opening statement, Warren Buffet spoke of every employee in the organisation becoming their own compliance officer. Still, going beyond compliance with rules, he asked his employees to follow a standard of conduct that does not bring them shame in front of their spouses, children and friends.

At its heart, Buffet's ask from his employees described an important principle: how would stakeholders with enough voice to get their issues broadcasted prominently in the mainstream and with sincere concerns about an organisation's externalities affect the organisation's reputation and the social standing of those who are a part of it?

As externalities are intrinsic to any business product, they need to be mapped for each diverse stakeholder. Stakeholders need to be asked in depth if they face or know of any externalities, 'pollution' or 'negative effects' due to a product or process of the organisation. Different stakeholders may have different externalities, and adding to the complexity, an externality for one stakeholder (harassment, hate, in social media) may be a core product (entertainment, information) for another. Hence, mapping the key product of a business used by the stakeholders and the externalities they face from the business helps to see if there are conflicts where a product for someone becomes an externality for someone else.

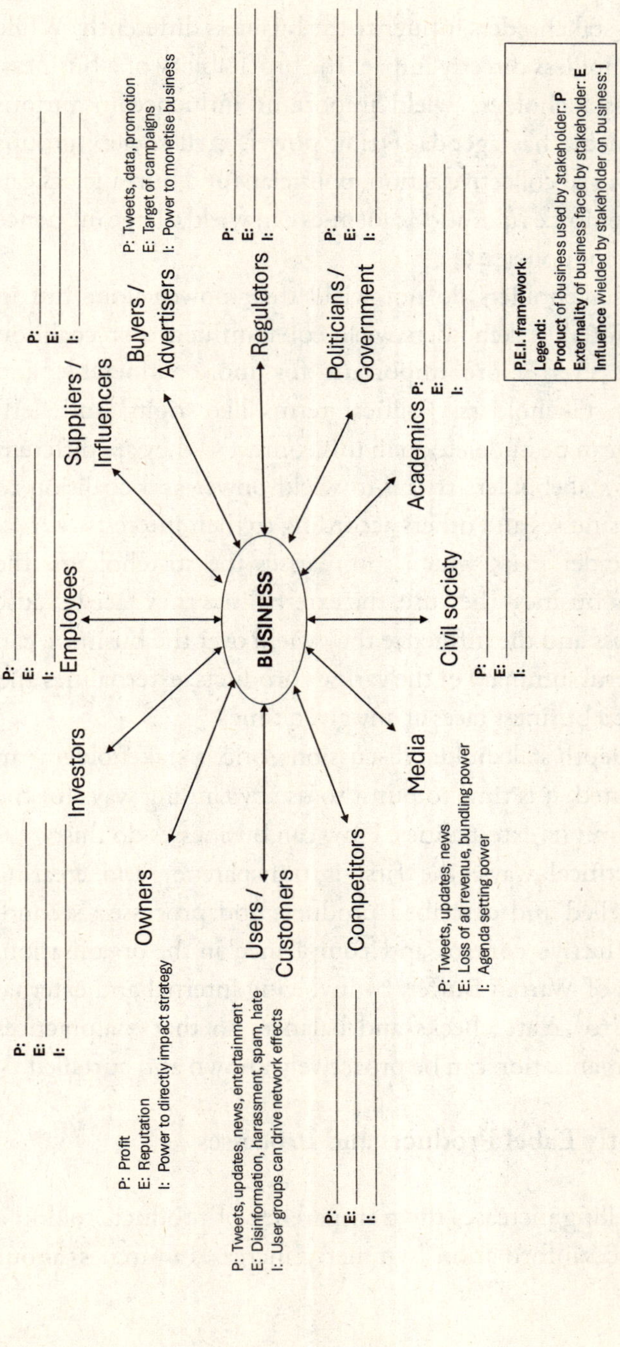

A stakeholder map, with products used and externalities faced by stakeholders, and their influence on the business.

Different stakeholders influence the business differently. While market stakeholders directly impact the profitability of a business, non-market stakeholders wield important influence in various ways. The media has agenda-setting power, civil society groups have the power of collective action, politicians and bureaucrats can legislate and enforce rules and academics can wield a large influence on the design of policies.

Usually, stakeholders do not wield their power alone but in coalitions. Not all stakeholders wield equal influence, so coalition formation is even more important for more vulnerable and marginalised stakeholders. Political terms like 'right' and 'left' wing groups can be understood in this context —they are different coalitions of stakeholders trying to wield power as a coalition to influence businesses and others according to their interests.

A stakeholder map, which summarises the stakeholders, the products of a business they use, the externalities they face because of the business and the influence they wield over the business, can provide a useful summary of the various products, externalities and tensions that a business faces at any given time.

After in-depth stakeholder discussions, once a stakeholder map has been created, it is time to put it to use by finding ways for the business to limit its externalities. How can businesses do this?

In two critical ways: the first is transparency and creating properly labelled and described products and processes; second, by putting effective 'control' and 'compliance' in the organisation, in the words of Warren Buffet, by involving internal and external stakeholders to create checks and balances so that malpractices within the organisation can be proactively known and curtailed.

Transparently Label Products and Processes

Product labelling increases the transparency of products sold in a market, reduces information asymmetry, increases awareness about externalities and reduces market failures. Hence, it remains one of the oldest forms of regulation.

Sometimes, labels are added voluntarily by businesses or industry associations (e.g., the Motion Picture Association film rating system in the US), at other times by government regulators (e.g., the rating of the Central Board of Film Certification in India) and at other times by strict government laws (such as on cigarette packaging).

While traditional labels have focused primarily on providing information about the product and its side effects to the user, labelling that informs users about the processes used in developing and manufacturing the product is increasingly included. For example, does a make-up product use animal testing? A dirty strategy is to include harmful labels in such a way that they do not catch the attention of the users. Regulators often push businesses to make labels more prominent, with cigarette packaging and its 'Smoking Kills' signs being prominent examples. However, in other cases, especially when business interests capture regulators, they may not push for such exhaustive labelling (e.g., in the chemicals industry).

Some practical and strategic questions must be resolved. Who should label products? Usually, businesses advocate for self-regulation through voluntary labelling (e.g., in the social media industry), while in more government-controlled economies, centralised regulation exists for such things. What regulatory option gets chosen can affect profitability and efficacy and decide which externalities get resolved for stakeholders. There is rarely a one-size-fits-all solution to regulation, as different stakeholders will prefer different regulatory options depending on their concerns and agenda.

Due to their advanced R&D, chemical companies like DuPont are often in the best position to discover the externalities associated with their products. However, can such a company be trusted with self-regulation and self-labelling if the penalties related to chemical pollution are not heavy and take decades to be levied? Can an industry consortium of chemical manufacturers (private centralised regulation) be expected to act more responsibly? In such a situation, a more centralised and public regulator seems attractive, but will it be safe from issues of regulatory capture, like a revolving door? In the case of social media content moderation, we will hesitate greatly to reach a similar conclusion. A centralised public regulator in the form of a censor or content moderation board will be highly controversial. A government regulator cannot not be trusted to label information responsibly and not use it for its propaganda.

The above questions reveal how the labelling and regulatory process is highly political and controversial, with stakeholders having different views. A valuable part of the stakeholder mapping exercise is understanding which stakeholders prefer what type of regulation / labelling for what kind of externality. Another approach that helps in the design process is understanding the costs and consequences of a particular labelling process on the various stakeholders.

Introduce Effective Checks and Balances

Can a labelling process ignore marginalised minorities? Developing a labelling process that ignores marginalised minorities and the externalities they face may be a cost-effective approach of the kind that DuPont embraced. If the consequences they bring to shareholders and the company are negligible, and if they don't have considerable influence in politics, media or civil society either to amplify their voice (seasonal migrants are one such stakeholder group), a purely calculative approach to strategy may argue that such marginalised minorities be ignored. Hence, deliberately ignoring externalities is often a 'profitable' approach by firms, as the monetary consequences of externalities on the business and their investors are minor compared to the benefits.[68] Firms with large and sophisticated legal teams can also find ways to legally justify such externalities unless explicit laws exist that criminalise withholding information about these externalities.

What is profitable and legal is not necessarily moral and responsible. When firms justify their actions in legal and financial terms instead of on parameters of responsible citizenship, it is a red flag about a firm's culture, governance and strategies. Calculating the monetary cost of externalities is intrinsically reprehensible. Can you put a price on the cancer caused by a business, even if there is a single victim? Imagine if justice functioned in this way, where each crime had a price, and criminals could just pay their way out of justice. Unfortunately, this system of justice still exists in many unregulated and uncompetitive (not free) markets, even in the world's most advanced economies. The 2008 financial crisis showcased this well, where large investment banks did not face any major legal consequences for their actions despite the dubious practices that perpetuated the *crisis*.

An empathetic design thinking approach to strategy emphasises the concerns of such marginalised minorities by putting them at the centre and viewing the weight of consequences from the stakeholders' shoes, not the narrow perspective of a manager or investor.

When Do Managers Act Responsibly?

We can classify three sources that govern manager decisions. First, *their values.* Are you comfortable with knowingly signing off on a decision or selling a product that involuntarily gives someone a lifelong medical condition or other debilitating externalities? Almost nobody would answer 'Yes' to this question. The follow-up question is more important: how far are you willing to go, as an individual manager, to sincerely learn from and inform the stakeholders about the externalities of your decisions and those of your business?

Second, the company's *internal governance*. Are there systems of checks and balances within the company that independently and continuously audit managers' decisions without the fear of backlash when these decisions hurt the bottom line and can challenge powerful decision-makers like the CEO and investors? A business with a system of checks and balances (which could be designed in many ways) and a democratic culture that values the voice of employees, community and, most importantly, whistleblowers is likelier to be nudged to take more responsible decisions.

Third, the *broader political economy*. What damages might a business have to pay if a decision made by the business causes publicly known externalities, and when? Such damages can come from various arenas: competitors, the judiciary, regulators, the political regime and, most saliently, the court of public opinion. Through various CSR (corporate social responsibility) and political activities (such as donations, lobbying, inducements, etc.), businesses attempt to influence these external stakeholders—politicians, bureaucrats, the legal system, the media, civil society groups and the public. They may also develop an interest in media ownership, which, neglecting editorial independence, can shape public opinion in critical moments in favour of the organisation.

When individual middle-level managers make tough decisions that involve externalities, they are likely to have little control over the broader political economy but can wield a greater influence on their firm's or department's internal governance. Integrating greater stakeholder engagement by giving them an authentic voice by documenting and transparently relaying their concerns and embedding design thinking processes when making decisions can radically transform the quality of our decisions.

Transparency and rigour in decision-making will seldom hurt a manager in companies driven by some ethical core. Nor will constructive and creative problem-solving not be valued by good organisations. An entrepreneurial and innovative manager who acts as a steward can turn threats into opportunities. For example, when a manager learns about the potential externalities of a product, they can engage with stakeholders, institute independent R&D on the externalities and solutions, and encourage open innovation to solve them rather than hide the information.

The stakeholder maps can help better understand how different stakeholders put checks and balances on each other in any given business or organisation. Beyond analysing how a stakeholder influences the business, one can also analyse how one stakeholder curbs or amplifies the influence of others. For example, even if workers do not have direct power to vote in shareholder-owned businesses, in most democracies, they have the formidable power to go on strike. In certain countries, like Scandinavian countries, workers have the explicit power of collective bargaining.

Stakeholder maps with a detailed analysis of how different stakeholders influence a business and each other and are influenced by them (products and externalities) can help designers understand the nature of power in a business. How power is distributed directly impacts how a business functions and the products and externalities the business produces.

By changing how stakeholders influence each other, the nature of business strategic decision-making can also be changed. Otherwise, without fundamental changes in the balance of power, the expectation that businesses will intrinsically change how they do business is toothless. Changes in this balance of power do not have to be through external and legislative regulation. Internal changes to the governance of business can also make businesses responsible.

***Hear the* ~~typicals~~ *atypicals*:**

- Design is not neutral, and who it is designed for is a strategic choice.
- Every product designed and sold has externalities, some of which are invisible.
- Atypical minorities help identify externalities and make organisations scientific and robust.
- Ignoring externalities increases public scrutiny, while ignoring the core product creates the risk of takeover.
- Mapping stakeholders, externalities and influence helps in robust atypical testing of organisations.

Rule 4

~~WIN~~ NURTURE

How would you like to be remembered?
'A person who made a difference. Not anything more, not anything less.'[69]

—Ratan Tata, Tata Sons

16

Public Goods Capitalism

Free enterprise rests on public goods, and public goods rest on a sense of community.

WE live in exceptional times in human history. Over two centuries, humanity has taken giant strides. Our lifespans have grown from an average of twenty-five (in 1800) to seventy-five. Infant mortality has plummeted from around 30 per cent to less than 3 per cent. A fact too often forgotten is how rapidly technology and quality of life for many has improved over the last few centuries. This rapid growth is called the hockey stick of progress, where people's per capita income grew exponentially, first in Western Europe and the United States, then in East Asia, and now in China and India.

The most immediate cause of this hockey stick growth was the Industrial Revolution, which began in the mid-eighteenth century, first in the United Kingdom. Economic historians have proposed several reasons for this revolution, almost all pointing towards the rapid technological advances that began to occur in Western Europe in the preceding centuries.

If we were to bet in the late fifteenth century which part of the world would be the richest in the subsequent centuries, very few would have said it would be countries at the western shore of Europe facing the Atlantic. Within Europe, it was Italy that was at the heart of culture and innovation. Beyond Europe, at its borders, Turkey was a formidable and increasingly powerful state that had captured and turned one of the greatest global cities, Constantinople, into its capital. China was a majestic empire at the forefront of several technological advancements—printing, paper money, gunpowder and more. India was the apple of the eye for most explorers, vying for a slice of its economy, the largest in the world.

Few would have bet on the English and the Dutch as future superpowers. However, something revolutionary was happening in the northwestern corner of Europe—the rise of free enterprise—which was about to change the region's and the world's fate.

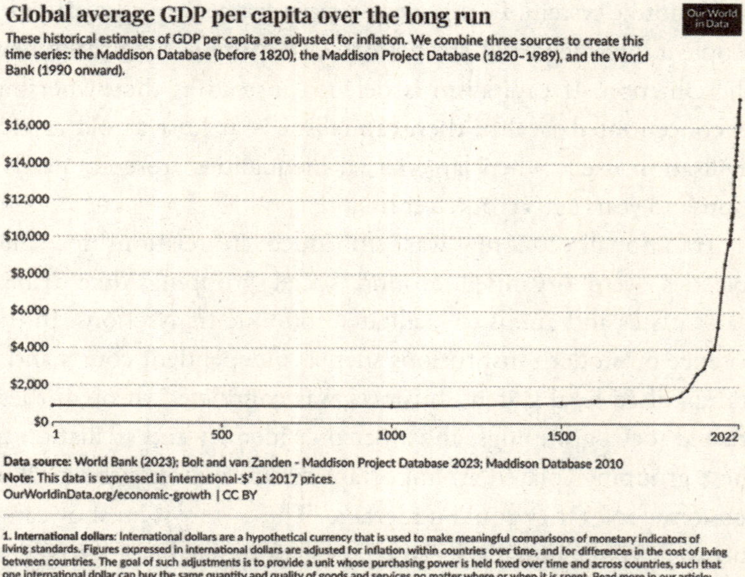

Hockey stick growth in the long run, in global average GDP per capital. Source: Our World in Data

History of Capitalism

Capitalism is an economic system that allows the private ownership of property.[70] Beyond this basic definition, capitalism holds different meanings for different people. For some, capitalism implies unrestricted free markets (laissez-faire); for others, it means free enterprise; and for others, it means disproportionate wealth in the hands of a few. To debate over which of the three truly defines capitalism is a fruitless taxonomical discussion. For this book, I define capitalism as this: capitalism is an economic system that allows individuals to freely enterprise in areas of their choosing.

If capitalism equals free enterprise, as a natural consequence, capitalism should be antithetical to cronyism and monopoly power. Ease of entry and exit in a market is the hallmark of such an economic system. In this view, a capitalist society that offers its people a high degree of freedom to enterprise is a relatively new phenomenon. If capitalism is defined instead as the ownership of concentrated wealth, then capitalism is at least as old as city civilisation itself, when large social inequalities arose about five thousand years ago across river basins.

Traditional economy was embedded in relationships, and societies were organised around social groupings like tribes, clans, castes and guilds to facilitate economic transactions. In the absence of modern institutions such as independent courts and a standardised legal system, business was conducted through these trusted social groupings, and a person's identity and affiliation to these groupings played an important role in defining the kind of economic roles they could undertake. The caste system showcased this well. While initially social stratification may have emerged as a result of occupational stratification, eventually a person's caste began to determine their traditional occupations, and women began to be largely excluded from economic life outside the household. These features were broadly true around the world.

The modern economy allows business to be conducted at arm's length. People perform long-distance exchanges with strangers, trusting that both parties are bound by laws, which, if broken, will bring punishment to the misbehaving parties. The modern economy is built on this rule of law. However, this rule of law did not emerge in a day or merely with the intentions of a benevolent ruler. It involved overcoming resistance from the incumbent 'capitalists'.

The medieval economy of Europe was dominated by the guild system, where guilds, city associations of traders (merchant guilds) and producers (craft guilds) enjoyed a monopoly over trade. Genoa's 'merchant' city was an exception to this monopolistic system, which followed free enterprise, and anyone could be a trader. While in the early second millennium these guilds were voluntary associations, over time, they became more exclusive, and a few traders / producers would dominate trade, and entry to the guild was highly controlled. Rulers would rely on these guilds for taxes, and hence, guilds enjoyed significant power in medieval European cities. As a result, rulers offered them exclusive monopoly rights, further strengthening the guilds' power.

In the sixteenth century, the power of merchant guilds began to decline as rulers stopped granting them monopolies and embraced freer enterprise with easier entry to outsiders in business. Cities like Amsterdam, Antwerp and London became some of the first centres of such free enterprise and, hence, the hubs of modern capitalist institutions. Amsterdam and London were among the first cities to develop stock exchanges (Amsterdam Stock Exchange in 1602, London Stock Exchange in 1698), while Antwerp developed a legendary commodities exchange (Antwerp Bourse in 1531). These cities were among the first to host joint stock companies like the British East India Company (1600) and the Dutch East India Company (1602). Other cities in Europe did not embrace such capitalist institutions. They continued to grant privileges to their merchant guilds until as late as the nineteenth century.

What motivated the cities in England and the Low Countries to embrace free enterprise? Moreover, were these free enterprise economies just a policy choice? For free enterprise to emerge in any region, it became essential that incumbent businesses of the region became comparatively less powerful, and the promise of attracting new entrants looked like a feasible pathway for raising taxation to the rulers of a city. Such conditions emerged for port cities on the Atlantic coast of Europe after 1500, when Atlantic trade and the trade with Asia through the Atlantic route opened a new world of economic possibilities for these regions, giving rise to English and Dutch traders in the north and Spanish and Portuguese traders in the south.

A Tale of Two Cities: Hamburg and Lübeck

The twin cities of Hamburg and Lübeck in northern Germany are just 65 kilometres apart, with Hamburg on the Atlantic coast and Lübeck on the Baltic. Both were key members of the medieval Hanseatic League, a federation of merchant guilds monopolising trade in northern Europe. Lübeck was the central Baltic trading hub and the Hanseatic's most powerful city, while Hamburg, its smaller cousin, provided the League access to the Atlantic. However, in the early modern period, the rise of Dutch traders disrupted their long-standing trade dominance. How did the two cities respond? Divergently. Lübeck responded by granting more privileges to its merchants and attempting to disrupt Dutch trade, while Hamburg eventually opened its trade to all, welcoming locals and foreigners.

This shift allowed Hamburg to integrate with the Atlantic trading system, attracting diverse merchants and expanding as a major Atlantic entrepôt. Lübeck, on the other hand, clung to its traditional privileges, hindering its ability to compete with the increasing foreign competition. As a result, Lübeck slowly declined, while Hamburg thrived by adapting to the new economic realities.

Opening up a city to free enterprise is not trivial. It involves creating a public contractual infrastructure[71] that can adjudicate inevitable conflict between business parties to support it. New accounting systems like double-entry bookkeeping in northwestern Europe were widely adopted during the early modern period. Additionally, there was an increase in keeping a written record in business, unlike in the past, when agreements were verbal. These innovations led to the rise of a legal system with public notaries and judiciary systems in cities like Amsterdam, Antwerp and London that could independently adjudicate conflicts and, hence, enjoy the legitimacy of various businesses. These northwest European port cities were also competing with each other to attract new businesses that wanted to benefit from the profitable Atlantic trade, and this competition made these cities invest even more in better contractual infrastructure.

Over time, new business forms began to emerge. Business became more formal, thanks to the adoption of formal accounting techniques and the emergence of public notaries that created a separation between work and home, where business became a legal entity—a 'firm'. Beyond individuals conducting business, formal partnerships emerged, where two or more people came together to run businesses according to the capital and effort invested.

At the end of the sixteenth century, another innovation began to emerge, which has been the hallmark of the modern capitalist system—joint stock companies. As businesses formalised, ownership over assets also became clearly defined. The notion of owning a 'share' in a business emerged as business became more formal and the accounting system became more sophisticated. So, over the sixteenth century, the idea of a joint stock company emerged in northwestern Europe.

As these formal modes of doing business emerged, with capital from multiple shareholders, they replaced smaller sustenance-based enterprises and older systems like merchant guilds. Modern firms had a better ability to scale up. Over the seventeenth century, large multinational joint stock companies rose: the East India Companies of the British and the Dutch. Unlike similar East India companies of Spain and Portugal, which were owned by the ruler, the British and Dutch companies were owned by the public, with their shares traded in the Amsterdam and London Stock Exchanges, acting as the direct predecessors of the modern public multinational corporations.

Importance of Public Goods and Commons

In all this, what is clear is that modern free enterprise capitalism could not have emerged without an enabling contractual infrastructure comprising a robust legal system and institutions such as the judiciary and law enforcement to implement and uphold this system in cases of conflict. For new businesses to thrive in a city like London, the legal system and its conflict resolution mechanisms needed to be perceived as fair and reliable. As a result, the legal systems in London were considered so equitable by the eighteenth century that during the Battle of Plassey in 1757 between Bengal Subah and the British East India Company, some Indian moneylenders ironically sided with the British, trusting that the strong British legal institutions would ensure the repayment of their loans.

If a fair public contractual infrastructure is so vital for the development of free enterprise capitalism, why is it not universally adopted? Often, this is because local incumbent businesses almost always enjoy strong political clout and oppose the widespread adoption of impartial legal systems that do not outright favour them. These entrenched interests prefer to maintain a status quo that gives them preferential treatment and protection from competition (e.g., Lübeck), thereby resisting reforms that would establish a more equitable legal framework.

Contractual infrastructure is a form of public good. Public goods have two unique characteristics. First, they are non-excludable, i.e., once they are provided, it is difficult or impossible to prevent people from using them. Second, public goods are non-rivalrous, i.e., one person's use does not reduce their availability to others. Contractual infrastructure, which includes a robust legal system, judiciary and law enforcement mechanisms, fits this definition well. Once established, contractual infrastructure benefits all participants in the economy by ensuring that contracts are enforceable and disputes can be resolved fairly.

Defence, clean water and public parks are classic examples of public goods. Defence forces protect all citizens within a country, and their provision for one person does not reduce their effectiveness for others. Clean water is another public good; once measures are taken to ensure water quality, everyone benefits from drinking it without diminishing its availability. Public parks offer recreational spaces that many can enjoy without depleting the resource. Other public goods include public roads, highways and bridges, and much of the public city infrastructure and facilities (e.g., libraries, museums), public schooling, universities, public health, public law and order, public broadcasting and environmental regulation.

Growth and Public Goods

Modern society and economy, including free enterprise capitalism, cannot exist without public goods. Economist Robert Lucas, in his explanation of the Industrial Revolution, cites London as an example, arguing that public goods like schooling allowed agricultural migrants from villages to settle in industrialising cities and enhance their own human capital and that of their children.[72] This leads to rapid advances in productivity (high human capital begets higher human capital), enabling a virtuous cycle of urbanisation, industrialisation and economic growth. Societies that failed to generate such public goods did not industrialise. Instead, they became cities like Dubai, where a vast immigrant population temporarily migrated to the city to serve the elites but failed to develop their skills and productivity to enhance such economies in the long run.

One of the most remarkable public goods is a library, which provides public access to a wealth of books and information to all public at no or nominal cost. Another remarkable public good is science—the research output from universities is publicly available at little to no cost to all, and this is especially free in the times of the internet, with the rise of open access and pre-print papers. Modern science and technological development could not exist without the emergence of science as a public activity and the public's access to affordable books through libraries in the post-printing-press revolution of the fifteenth century. For example, economic historian Joel Mokyr discusses the role of the Republic of Letters, an informal pan-European network of scientists and intellectuals, in developing early modern science.[73] In an open network, scientists and intellectuals shared their latest works, commented on each other and built on the work of others through letter writing, laying the groundwork for modern science. Another example of such public goods was the *Encyclopédie*. This eighteenth-century (1751) French encyclopaedia brought together prominent scientists and scholars from different fields to create a common and succinct body of knowledge for public consumption.

The patent system, enforced by the State, is also part of public goods. It aims to balance the interests of private innovators to earn profits on their R&D investments and public benefit by making scientific and technological knowledge publicly available. As discussed earlier, the patent system does so by granting temporary monopolies to innovators in return for public disclosure of their innovations. Fruits of scientific progress—general purpose technologies like steam and IC engines, electricity, the internet and AI—are public goods, and anyone anywhere can benefit from them.

Another term related to public goods is 'commons', which are non-excludable goods that are rivalrous, i.e., goods which anyone can use but get depleted with overuse. Groundwater is a good example of commons. While everyone benefits from groundwater, overuse by one or many households and businesses can deplete it. Forests, fisheries and most natural resources are commons. Not all natural resources are owned as commons, however. Some natural resources are privately held (e.g., land) and used for the private benefit of the owners.

A healthy debate exists over which and how much of the earth's resources should be privately held. The standard socialist argument against private ownership of natural resources is that they are the earth's bounty to all, not just a few. The argument for private ownership—the capitalist argument—is that publicly held natural resources can be overused, and privately held natural resources can instead be used optimally to maximise returns from them. Different countries and political ideologies within the same countries (e.g., Tories vs Conservatives in the UK) hold different views on this topic, and it becomes an important theme during elections.

The Contagion of Free-riding

Public goods and commons are at the heart of any healthy society. However, public goods are not easy to produce, and commons are often at risk of overuse and depletion. The non-excludable nature of public goods and commons, which greatly benefits all, also acts as a curse for their production and use. This inherent paradox leads to the under-production of public goods and a 'tragedy of the commons'.

The *public goods dilemma* is the problem of under-production, which is characteristic of public goods. All public goods, whether defence, public infrastructure or public knowledge, require contributions from the public—either in the form of taxation, when these goods are publicly provided, or else in the form of donations (e.g., the Islamic *zakat*), when these goods are provided by others like religious or business organisations (e.g., gurdwaras, the Tatas). However, as public goods benefit all, and the benefits cannot be tied to just those who pay for these public goods, it creates a possibility for free riding—'This facility is available to me anyway. Let me not contribute to it this time'—and evasion: 'I suspect my neighbours did not pay their taxes fully, and instead bought a luxury car. Why are we foolishly paying the road taxes when others are free riding? Let us also pay less tax and buy a luxury car instead and enjoy the roads we paid for so diligently all these years.'

Scientific innovation benefits all and requires the contributions of several innovators to a common pool of knowledge (e.g., GitHub or Wikipedia). However, an innovator may think, 'Many take ideas from the pool of knowledge I contribute to but do not give back. Let me also not share my ideas, as it seems like I am the chicken making unnecessary sacrifices when others just free ride.' Free riding, such as tax evasion, littering, disposing of waste in rivers or not contributing to a common pool, can become endemic in the whole population, where free riding by one motivates free riding by others, leading to an under-provision of public goods. Seeing piles of garbage in a scenic neighbourhood results from such a self-fulfilling prophecy: 'Others are throwing garbage here, and I alone cannot clean this, so let me just throw my garbage here as well.'

The tragedy of the commons stems from a similar problem of overuse of the commons. While everyone benefits from a high ground water table, if anyone can drill a borewell and draw a little extra water (free ride) out of the groundwater resource beyond levels that can be replenished, it can lead to rapid depletion of groundwater, hurting everyone, including the over-user. However, once one person finds out that someone else is free riding and drawing more water than they should, leaving less for them, they also get incentivised to free ride, thinking, 'Our neighbours are drawing four times the amount of water than they should, and I am the only one being responsible. If we continue this way, we will have much less water left to use. So we must also increase our groundwater use, even if it is tragic that we are in this place.' This contagion of free riding could lead to a race to the bottom and rapid depletion of the commons.

Free riding may seem like an attractive alternative in the short term for individuals when they see the world from their self-centred view. However, when freeriding becomes endemic, it becomes a very expensive tragedy to be in. Healthcare in India is a good example. With a very small tax base, public healthcare[74] in India is chronically underfunded, translating into expensive and often unreliable private healthcare and poor public health, leading to diseases like dengue and jaundice. The same can be said about many other services in India: underfunding of civic amenities leads to expensive private sourcing of essential utilities like water, and underfunding of public education leads to expensive private schooling and universities. Such free riding is also behind environmental degradation across many parts of the world, especially the mountainous regions like the Himalayas, where natural resources are rampantly overused at a rate that far exceeds replenishment, leading to short-term gain in footfalls, but long-term damage to not just the environment but also the locals, their quality of life and their economy.

European countries, especially Scandinavian nations, are noted for their high-quality public goods provision, which dramatically improves life quality. The under-provision of public goods not only leads to lower quality of life for everyone, including the rich (who may be just as much at risk of diseases such as malaria due to poor public health) but also perpetuates inequality and makes it difficult for the poor to escape the poverty trap. Once a culture of free riding sets in in a society, it is self-perpetuating, leading to underprovided public goods and depleted commons, as for example in public health: 'Why would I get treatment in poor public hospitals when I can afford to go to good private hospitals? And why should I pay high taxes to fund public hospitals, when I have to spend so much of my hard-earned money to get private healthcare?'

Privatisation that locks out the poor from many basic services like healthcare, education and amenities may also be called capitalism. However, it represents a peculiar form of capitalism devoid of community and equality of opportunity, which are central to a truly free enterprise capitalism, where anyone can bootstrap and succeed with enterprise and innovation. Hence, free enterprise capitalism needs healthy public goods and commons and is thus grounded in a sense of community.

The idea of a business focused narrowly on profit maximisation, divorced from the responsibility of giving back to the commons, is antithetical to the spirit of free enterprise capitalism. Public goods capitalism, which emphasises the centrality of public goods and commons in the functioning of a free enterprise economy and lays the responsibility of providing these goods on all economic actors, especially those who are its greatest beneficiaries, is all the more important as the world faces challenges like global warming.

Example	Type	
Defence	Public goods	Non-excludable and non-rivalrous; all citizens are protected by a nation's defence, and protection for one person does not reduce protection for others

Example	Type	
Clean water	Public goods	Non-excludable and non-rivalrous once it's purified; everyone benefits from drinking water, and one person's consumption does not diminish the quality for others
Public parks	Public goods	Non-excludable and non-rivalrous; everyone can access public parks without depleting the resource for others
Libraries	Public goods	Non-excludable and non-rivalrous; anyone can access books and information, and one person's use doesn't reduce the availability for others
Science	Public goods	Non-excludable and non-rivalrous; scientific knowledge, particularly open access, benefits all and doesn't diminish with use
Public roads / highways	Public goods	Non-excludable and non-rivalrous; once built, they benefit everyone, and one person's use doesn't reduce access for others (unless congested)
Education	Public goods	Non-excludable and non-rivalrous when publicly provided; once available, education enhances human capital without reducing availability to others

Example	Type	
Groundwater	Commons	Non-excludable but rivalrous; anyone can use groundwater, but overuse by some depletes the resource for others
Forests	Commons	Non-excludable but rivalrous; open access to forests can lead to overuse and depletion, reducing availability for future users
Fisheries	Commons	Non-excludable but rivalrous; anyone can fish, but overfishing depletes the stock, limiting future availability
Public healthcare	Public goods	Non-excludable and non-rivalrous; benefits everyone by reducing disease and improving public health, even if they do not directly contribute to it
Public knowledge (e.g., Wikipedia)	Public goods	Non-excludable and non-rivalrous; shared knowledge is available to all and doesn't get depleted by use
Public broadcasting	Public goods	Non-excludable and non-rivalrous; everyone can access public broadcasting without diminishing its quality or availability
Patent system	Public goods	Temporary monopolies for innovators in exchange for public disclosure of innovations, benefiting everyone in the long run with new technologies and knowledge

17

The Future of Business

The modern corporation, with its narrow shareholder focus, may not survive in the new world.

SINCE the last few decades, there has been an uptake in the concept of 'philanthrocapitalism'. Wealthy business owners like Bill and Melinda Gates, Warren Buffet and Mark Zuckerberg have made large donations to public charities as part of the Giving Pledge, motivating others to join and give away at least half of their wealth to independent philanthropies. American oil magnate John D. Rockefeller and steel magnate Andrew Carnegie pioneered this philanthropic approach to capitalism in the early twentieth century, when they gave large portions of their wealth to the eponymous Rockefeller and Carnegie Foundations.

Philanthrocapitalism?

Can philanthrocapitalism be the future of business and capitalism? No. While several external market, non-market and regulatory mechanisms exist to limit dirty strategies businesses may deploy to make money, what strong and binding internal controls can limit incentives for businesses to pursue dirty strategies? The predominant philosophy of businesses is shareholder capitalism, where the primary vision of a business is to make profits for shareholders. How can such a business not stray towards amoral drift?

Philanthrocapitalism, where business is separate from philanthropy, such as Carnegie's and Rockefeller's businesses, is charitable. However, it has no solutions for restricting businesses from pursuing dirty strategies. Philanthrocapitalism can worsen dirty strategies, if it becomes an excuse for wealthy business owners to pursue dirty strategies in their business domain and then (later) use philanthropy for reputation laundering to improve their business and personal legacy.

It is worth highlighting that businesses with some of the worst environmental or social responsibility records have large associated philanthropies. Erstwhile US pharmaceutical giant Purdue Pharma offers a cautionary tale. A leading pharmaceutical company, it became infamous in the 2010s for its role in the opioid drug crisis in the US. The company aggressively marketed OxyContin, a highly addictive painkiller, while downplaying its risk of addiction. This strategy contributed to the widespread opioid epidemic, leading to hundreds of thousands of overdose deaths and leaving countless individuals struggling with addiction. Despite knowing the addictive nature of OxyContin, Purdue Pharma continued to push its sales.[75] This unethical behaviour ultimately led to numerous lawsuits against the company, culminating in Purdue Pharma filing for bankruptcy in 2019.

Despite the controversies surrounding Purdue Pharma, the Sackler family, who owned the company, became notable philanthropists, donating millions to prestigious cultural and educational institutions that displayed the family name in recognition of their donations. However, as the extent of Purdue

Pharma's unethical practices came to light, these donations faced increased scrutiny, with many institutions reevaluating their ties to the Sackler name.

Rockefeller and Carnegie were infamous for their monopolistic practices, using various strategies to crush competition and labour. For example, Rockefeller formed a secret alliance (a cabal) with major railway businesses to secure rebates for his company, Standard Oil. This scheme allowed him to undercut rivals and gain control over the oil market. Carnegie, similarly, is infamous for the Homestead Strike of 1892, where his management crushed striking workers through the violent use of hired armed agents. Although great philanthropists, the two business magnates are hence viewed as cautionary examples of 'robber baron' crony capitalism. Their legacy improved significantly later with their generous philanthropy.

Philanthropy can also become a way for business owners to capture non-market stakeholders. Wealthy business owners and their philanthropies are a source of potential funding for non-market stakeholders—from NGOs to universities—and such stakeholders may be unwilling to be critical of their wealthy connections, fearing pushback with financial consequences. Additionally, such donations can be used to establish captured think tanks or academic positions that advocate for policies or conduct research that promotes the donor's business interests.

Purdue Pharma is a cautionary example of this too, among other opioid manufacturers.[76] Purdue gave large donations to promote the 'science behind the use' of opioids in pain management. For instance, it made significant financial contributions to institutions like Tufts University and Massachusetts General Hospital. At Tufts, Purdue funded the establishment of the Sackler Graduate School of Biomedical Sciences and supported programmes like the Master's in Pain Research, Education and Policy. The influence of these donations extended to the development of curricula and research that favoured opioid prescription, downplaying the risks of addiction and overuse.

This financial support also reached professional societies and patient advocacy organisations. The American Pain Society and the American Academy of Pain Medicine, both recipients of Purdue funding, played crucial roles in developing guidelines and educational materials that minimised the potential for addiction, which healthcare professionals widely adopted. These organisations, along with the US Pain Foundation and others, became key players in shaping public and professional perceptions of opioid use.

If businesses are primarily motivated to pursue dirty strategies for profits, philanthropies associated with them may also become a tool for reputation laundering or, worse, an instrument of capture. Hence, it is necessary to explore business structures that can offer strong internal controls within businesses that limit the ability of businesses to pursue dirty strategies.

Economic Democracy?

Examining the various types of ownership forms prevalent today in business can help us answer the question of the future of ownership. Some of the most commonly found business forms include the *private limited company*, such as the agricultural giant US Cargill, which is owned by a small group of private shareholders; the *limited liability partnerships*, such as the professional services company Deloitte, which is owned by various partners who share the profits of the business; and the *publicly listed company*, such as Indian FMCG giant ITC, whose shares are owned by various investors and traded in stock markets. Additionally, there can be cooperatives: *producer-owned organisations* such as the Indian dairy giant Amul, where farmers cooperatively own the business, and *employee-owned companies* such as the British retailer John Lewis Partnership. Additionally, many businesses are *state-owned enterprises* primarily owned by the state, such as the petroleum giant Saudi Aramco, and India's public sector units (PSUs), such as Steel Authority of India Limited and Coal India.

Beyond these basic organisational forms, it is also useful to consider who controls the company, especially in large businesses. *Family-controlled businesses* are an important subgroup of businesses, with companies like Reliance (Ambani family) and Walmart (Walton family) being prominent examples. Then we also have higher business forms, such as *business groups* (e.g., Tata Group, Korean chaebols) that are closely working businesses, often with a shared brand with common ownership, often found in developing countries; and *conglomerates* (e.g., Berkshire Hathaway) which are a group of diversified businesses with common ownership. Another distinct business form is the *keiretsu*, which are common in Japan (e.g., Mitsubishi) where a group of businesses have cross-holding in each other, forming a close alliance.

Type	Ownership and control	Purpose and governance	Example and explanation
Private limited company	Owned by a small group of private shareholders	Focus on growth and privacy; governance includes a board of directors, often family or founders	**Cargill (USA)**: Owned by the Cargill and MacMillan families, maintaining control and confidentiality, focusing on growth and strategies without public market pressures

Type	Ownership and control	Purpose and governance	Example and explanation
Limited liability partnership (LLP)	Owned by partners with limited liability	Facilitate professional collaboration; shared management responsibilities	**Deloitte (Global)**: Partners share in the firm's profits while limiting personal liability, offering flexibility and balancing collaboration with risk
Publicly listed company	Owned by public shareholders, traded on stock exchanges	Maximise shareholder value; governed by a board of directors accountable to shareholders	**Apple (USA)**: Publicly traded on NASDAQ, raising capital through public investment, emphasising innovation and shareholder returns
Employee-owned company	Owned by employees through stock ownership	Enhance motivation through shared ownership; employee participation in governance	**John Lewis Partnership (UK)**: Owned by employees who share in profits and participate in decision-making, enhancing engagement, motivation, and loyalty

Type	Ownership and control	Purpose and governance	Example and explanation
Producer-owned organisation	Combines social and financial ownership structures	Achieve financial and social objectives; balances profit motives with social goals	**Amul (India)**: A cooperative organisation focusing on empowering dairy farmers and enhancing their economic status while providing quality dairy products
State-owned enterprise (SOE)	Owned and operated by the government	Serve public and strategic national interests; managed by government-appointed leadership	**Saudi Aramco (Saudi Arabia)**: Fully owned by the Saudi government, reflecting strategic importance to national interests and energy policy, aligning operations with government objectives

Type	Ownership and control	Purpose and governance	Example and explanation
Family-controlled business	Majority control by a family	Balance family legacy with business growth; family members in key roles, possibly including professional managers	**Walmart (USA)**: Controlled by the Walton family, focusing on long-term growth and sustaining the family's legacy in retail leadership
Business group	Collection of businesses under a common administrative or financial control	Shared resources and strategic planning across businesses, often with a central holding company	**Tata Group (India)**: Encompasses numerous companies across sectors like steel, automotive and technology, allowing for shared resources and strategic alignment under the Tata brand

Type	Ownership and control	Purpose and governance	Example and explanation
Keiretsu	Networks of interlinked businesses with cross-shareholding	Mutual growth and stability through shared resources and cooperation	**Mitsubishi Group (Japan)**: Consists of affiliated companies across sectors like finance and industrial products, maintaining strong ties and coordinated business strategies
Conglomerate	Owns diverse businesses across industries	Diversify risk and resources; centralised management with decentralised operations	**Berkshire Hathaway (USA)**: Owns a diverse range of businesses, from insurance to manufacturing, enabling risk diversification and capital allocation

Among these various business forms, the cooperative is the form of business that has been proposed for a long time as an alternative to shareholder-centric business models, where different stakeholders (primarily employees or producers) have a sizeable democratic say in the functioning of the business. How much stakeholder democracy can a business allow? Should decisions be made via consensus and participation, or should they be hierarchical, focusing on implementation? Businesses showcase a wide variety on this issue.

At its core, a business is a production system that takes *capital* (e.g., cows and machines), *labour* and *skills* to create a product or service with a certain degree of efficiency (also called TFP). An economy is an aggregate of all such production. There are, hence, three fundamental stakeholders in any production function—the capitalists (who own capital), the workers (who exert labour with a certain skill level) and a complex web of stakeholders (internal managers and professionals and external ecosystem players that influence efficiency).

Businesses are usually capital-owned, i.e., owned by their shareholders (capitalists), who elect a board that then appoints a CEO, the manager who runs the firm on their behalf. Businesses can also be labour-owned and owned by workers or producers. An example of a worker-owned cooperative is the John Lewis Partnership, owning popular retail brands John Lewis and Waitrose in the UK. An example of a producer-owned organisation is dairy behemoth Amul in India. Producer cooperatives also bring in capital. An analysis of forty-seven cooperatives and fifty-four publicly listed companies by McKinsey[77] showed that both grew at similar rates between 2005 and 2010. In such coops, the final authority rests with the workers / producers, who usually elect a governing board that appoints a CEO to run the daily affairs of the business.

Cooperatives and modern corporations are diametrically opposite in terms of who owns the company. However, even within capital-owned businesses, there can be great diversity in the autonomy managers and workers enjoy vs. owners. Firms with better corporate governance restrict the day-to-day intervention of an owner in a company's affairs through a system of checks and balances, as a company and its owners are two separate legal entities. In other instances, founders of a business can enjoy a more significant say in decision-making (by owning Class A shares) even if their actual share of stocks in the company has been diluted with further external investment. Such innovations (classes of shares) can also be implemented in principle in cooperatives if they ever go for public listing to raise funds, where workers may have a privileged position within the firm like founders in many modern corporations.

Often, shareholder-owned businesses are good at risk-taking, a critical aspect of business-building, with legal innovations like limited liability partnerships (LLP) helping such risk-takers even further. Shareholder-owned businesses are also better at raising external capital, which cooperatives are known to struggle with, and they resort to bank loans as some of the few viable sources of capital. Pure cooperatives, which are entirely worker-owned, have a significant but limited scope of operations (in industries like agriculture, banking and retail).

In many emerging industries, the distinction between capital-owned and labour-owned organisations has begun to blur with the emerging popularity of employee stock ownership plans (ESOPs), especially in the start-up ecosystem, in which business-critical employees, and especially the first founding employees of a business, get share ownership in the business, negotiated as part of their remuneration. Centi-billionaire Steve Ballmer is a good example—the erstwhile CEO of Microsoft was the thirtieth employee of Microsoft and the first business hire, who held 8 per cent shares of Microsoft at incorporation.

Different stakeholders—investors, founders, employees and even suppliers or buyers—can negotiate different shares for themselves in new ventures, and the natural rise of such negotiated shareholding has created the scope for a more significant say for various stakeholders. However, such negotiated shareholding has little to no scope for non-market stakeholders. So, such new business forms can still suffer from the same challenges as traditional businesses, where they do not consider the full effects of negative externalities on their surrounding communities and pursue dirty strategies that hurt communities.

Chapter 18

Philanthropy-owned Businesses

A future may be businesses owned by charities; they have a history of commercial success and social good.

ACADEMICS and business practitioners worldwide grapple with a grand challenge of our times—how do we integrate community and business, such that businesses can be internally motivated to contribute to their communities. Philanthrocapitalism, although charitable, has no solutions to the conflict between the visionless pursuit of profit and the harms it can have on our public goods and commons. Similarly, worker democracy, an enticing idea gaining ground through the rise of negotiated shareholding in new ventures, empowers many workers. However, it still does not offer a way to include the community. *How can a Madagascar family suffering from the ill effects of famine have a seat at the tables where decisions that affect them are made?*

Very few businesses like the Tatas have embodied a spirit of giving back throughout their long history. We have discussed the Tatas and their grounded approach to business at length. It is worthwhile to revisit the organisation to understand the singular organisational form that gives the company a unique character.

The Tata Group is India's largest conglomerate, with a combined revenue of $165 billion and employing nearly a million people. It comprises multiple publicly traded multi-billion-dollar businesses across industries from steel to EV, with its parent company, Tata Sons, as its principal shareholder. Tata Sons itself is a private investment holding company that is majorly owned (66 per cent) by Tata Trusts, a group of philanthropic organisations with a history going as far back as 1892 with the foundation of the J.N. Tata Endowment. The many nation-building contributions of Tata Trusts include setting up national institutions like the Indian Institute of Science (IISc in 1909), Tata Institute of Social Sciences (TISS in 1936), Tata Memorial Hospital (in 1941), Tata Medical Centre (in 2011) and the National Cancer Grid (in 2012), contributing to education and healthcare in India.

Such a direct and *controlling* ownership of a large business by one or a group of philanthropic organisations (called enterprise foundations) represents a unique ownership structure pioneered by the Tatas in India. It has gained some popularity over the past century, especially in Northern Europe. Danish alcoholic beverages company Carlsberg and German optics multinational Carl Zeiss were a few other pioneering businesses like Tata that were vested in the hands of philanthropies in the nineteenth century (Carlsberg in 1876, Carl Zeiss in 1889).

Some other large businesses that have a similar *enterprise foundation* ownership arrangement include American chocolate multinational Hershey, Danish pharmaceutical giant Novo Nordisk, British newspaper *The Guardian*, the legendary Swiss watchmaker Rolex, German engineering multinational Bosch, and Swedish furniture giant IKEA. Indian IT consultancy giant Wipro could also be on its way to a similar model, where Wipro's majority owner, Azim Premji, has transferred much of his wealth to the philanthropic Azim Premji Foundation.

Business	Area of business, revenue and size (FY23-24)	Enterprise foundation	Founding story
Carlsberg	Alcoholic beverages (Denmark), ~$10 billion, 30,000 employees	Carlsberg Foundation	Founded by J.C. Jacobsen in 1847 in Copenhagen, Denmark. Jacobsen established the foundation in 1876 to support scientific research and public education.
Carl Zeiss	Optics and optoelectronics (Germany), ~$11 billion, 46,000 employees	Carl Zeiss Foundation	Founded by Carl Zeiss in 1846 in Jena, Germany. Ernst Abbe established the foundation in 1889 to reinvest profits into research and education.

Business	Area of business, revenue and size (FY23-24)	Enterprise foundation	Founding story
Tata Group	Conglomerate (India), ~$165 billion, 1 million employees	Tata Trusts	Founded by Jamsetji Tata in 1868 in India. Tata established the endowment in 1892, which evolved into the trusts, to support education, healthcare and livelihoods.
The Hershey Company	Confectionery (USA), ~$9 billion, 21,000 employees	Milton Hershey School Trust	Founded by Milton S. Hershey in 1894 in Pennsylvania, USA. Hershey established the trust in 1909 to fund and operate a school for orphaned boys.

Business	Area of business, revenue and size (FY23-24)	Enterprise foundation	Founding story
Novo Nordisk	Pharmaceuticals (Denmark), ~$32 billion, 64,000 employees	Novo Nordisk Foundation	Founded by August Krogh, Marie Krogh and Hans Christian Hagedorn in 1923 in Denmark. The foundation was established in 1924 to support healthcare and research.
The Guardian	Newspaper (United Kingdom), ~$332 million, 1,200 employees	Scott Trust Limited	Founded by John Edward Taylor in 1821 as *The Manchester Guardian*, the newspaper came under the ownership of the Scott Trust in 1936 to safeguard its editorial independence.

Business	Area of business, revenue and size (FY23-24)	Enterprise foundation	Founding story
Rolex	Watchmaking (Switzerland), ~$10 billion, 30,000 employees	Hans Wilsdorf Foundation	Founded by Hans Wilsdorf and Alfred Davis in 1905 in London, England. Wilsdorf established the foundation in 1945 to support charitable causes, especially education and entrepreneurship.
Bosch	Engineering and electronics (Germany), ~$96 billion, 430,000 employees	Robert Bosch Stiftung	Founded by Robert Bosch in 1886 in Stuttgart, Germany. The foundation was established in 1964 to support health, science, education and international relations projects.

Business	Area of business, revenue and size (FY23-24)	Enterprise foundation	Founding story
IKEA	Furniture (Sweden), ~$47 billion, 155,000 employees	Stichting INGKA Foundation	Founded by Ingvar Kamprad in 1943 in Sweden. Kamprad established the foundation in 1982 to support architecture, interior design and sustainable living initiatives.

Enterprise foundations like Tata Trusts and the Novo Nordisk Foundation are distinct from independent philanthropies such as the Gates Foundation and the Ford Foundation, which have been significantly funded by wealthy donors (Bill and Melinda Gates and the Ford family) associated with founding major corporations like Microsoft and Ford. Enterprise foundations are also different from philanthropies like the Coca-Cola Foundation and the Reliance Foundation, which their respective corporations directly own.

Enterprise foundations are unique because they are philanthropies that own businesses, enabling them to influence the objectives and operations of these enterprises directly.[78] Such philanthropy-owned businesses are insulated from the risks of amoral drift as they are unlikely to be susceptible to hostile takeovers. Hence, they have been found to focus on long-term strategic planning characterised by fiscal conservatism instead of short-termism.[79] They also have been found to have better reputation and social responsibility ratings, with a strong focus on employee welfare, stable employment practices, better wages and longer tenure.[80] Given a more holistic approach to business, these businesses are found to perform just as well financially and in the stock market, if not better, enjoying more stable earnings and higher survival rates.[81]

If enterprise foundations have such benefits, why are they not more common? Despite a long global history of enterprise foundations, Denmark is the only country where enterprise foundations are the dominant ownership form, comprising more than half of the country's entire market capitalisation.[82] Family-controlled businesses (like Reliance) and individually-controlled businesses (like Wipro) may reach a point where they can turn their businesses into foundations by passing on their shares to philanthropy. However, bestowing the ownership of a company to philanthropy, which is not owned by any person or group but is rather independent and self-governed by a set of codes and a board, is a major act of charity. If the Tatas were less charitable, they and their children could have been some of the wealthiest individuals in the world. Instead, the various charities named after the Tatas are wealthy.

In many cultures, passing down wealth from one generation to another as inheritance is considered a parental or family duty, and such a sense of duty may deter many from taking the philanthropic route. Countries like Denmark and other North European nations have become culturally more open to the idea of individual responsibility—that parents do not owe a large fortune to their children. Hence, passing the ownership of a business to philanthropy instead of the family may not appear like a transgression of social expectations in North European culture. Such cultural attitudes, where children do not feel entitled to the wealth of their parents and have a sense of individual autonomy, are more likely to foster enterprise foundations, passing the ownership of businesses to philanthropies instead of children.

Another factor limiting enterprise foundations in countries like the US is the general legal and regulatory scepticism towards ownership structures that fuse together profit with philanthropy. In the US, profit-driven businesses are taxed while philanthropies are not, leading to the view that such foundations would neither be good philanthropies nor good businesses, but rather a way for businesses to evade taxes (e.g., the 1969 US Tax Reform Act that effectively banned enterprise foundations in the US). Such regulatory hurdles led foundations like the Ford Foundation to become independent charities rather than the enterprise foundations they were initially envisioned to be.

Although financially sound and attractive performers in the stock market, philanthropy-owned organisations may find it challenging to raise capital quickly because the controlling stake held by philanthropic entities can limit the ability of the business to dilute ownership.[83] This is a unique challenge not just for philanthropy-owned organisations but also for any business with controlling shareholders. There have been cases where philanthropy-owned businesses divested themselves or diluted their stake. For example, the British pharmaceutical giant Burroughs Wellcome eventually merged with Glaxo and SmithKline Beecham to form the pharma giant now known as GlaxoSmithKline. The associated enterprise foundation Wellcome Trust divested itself from the pharma business in 1995, and today, it is one of the world's largest philanthropies focused on healthcare research, being one of the largest funders of science in the world.

Since philanthropy-owned businesses resist takeovers, investors looking to gain controlling ownership or influence its strategic direction may be discouraged, slowing the pace at which these businesses raise capital. Because the vision of the business is deeply embedded in the organisation due to its ownership structure, it is unlikely that such businesses can be quickly taken over and steered in a different strategic direction by another shareholder.

While the validity of the above concerns must be appreciated, there is another way to view the issue. Businesses with a strong vision that does not prioritise profit maximisation alone will always be less attractive to short-term investors and, hence, unlikely to get quick capital. However, is that necessarily a disadvantage for businesses if it protects them from amoral drift away from their social mission? This becomes especially relevant given that research by management scholars like Steen Thomsen and long-term investor confidence in businesses such as Tata shows that philanthropy-owned businesses are financially sound as well as socially responsible.

19

What Good Can Businesses Do?

From scientific innovation to last-mile connectivity, there are many ways in which businesses can create commons.

In this book, we have spoken at length about the negative externalities of businesses. Conversely, what are some of the positive side effects that businesses can create for society? There are several.

Innovation at the Frontier

Businesses are hubs of innovation, and this is often their greatest strength. Some of the most important scientific and technological innovations have emerged from the industry. Fifty Nobel Prize-winning discoveries, including 11 per cent of all physics (4–6 per cent in medicine and chemistry) prizes, occurred in the industry, with organisations such as the legendary R&D laboratory Bell Labs (owned by US telecom giant AT&T, now Nokia) and US technology giant IBM being prime examples.[84]

Several technologies such as vacuum tubes, transistors, integrated circuits, fibre optics, lasers, LED and now AI, that have been foundational in the development of the modern digital age could not have been possible without the fundamental contributions of scientists working within or closely with the industry.

The invention of the vacuum tube in 1904 by British scientist John Ambrose Fleming at the British telecom giant Marconi Company—founded by the Italian inventor Guglielmo Marconi, known for pioneering early radio technology—heralded the computer age. Vacuum tubes, crucial for the development of computers, were later significantly improved by the US conglomerate General Electric, founded by Thomas Edison, the renowned inventor of the light bulb. These devices were instrumental in developing the earliest computers, in which IBM (e.g., its Harvard Mark I 1944) played a pioneering role, until their limitations in size and reliability spurred further innovation.

In 1947, scientists John Bardeen, Walter Brattain and William Shockley made a breakthrough at Bell Labs by developing the transistor. Transistors made electronic devices smaller, more reliable and more energy-efficient, setting the stage for the miniaturisation of electronics. This led to the development of integrated circuits (ICs) by Jack Kilby at Texas Instruments in 1958 and independently by Robert Noyce at Fairchild Semiconductor in 1959. ICs combined multiple electronic components into single chips, facilitating the creation of complex microprocessors that fuelled the computer revolution, spearheaded by organisations such as IBM and US semiconductor major Intel.

The internet has been developing in parallel since the 1960s, and its widespread use by the 1990s required the development of better data transmission technologies. Engineer Charles K. Kao at Standard Telecommunication Laboratories, part of the British telecom major Standard Telecommunication Company, revolutionised the field in 1966 by demonstrating that glass fibres could transmit light and, hence, data over long distances with minimal loss, creating the backbone of today's internet and telecom infrastructure. The development of the laser made additional contributions to this growth. Initially proposed by Albert Einstein in 1917, Theodore Maiman initiated the actual development of lasers at Hughes Aircraft in 1960, with significant theoretical contributions from researchers at Bell Labs, such as Arthur Schawlow and Charles Townes.

The development of modern digital devices also required better and more portable displays, which today operate on light-emitting diodes (LEDs). Nick Holonyak Jr. conducted initial research at General Electric and developed the first practical LED in 1962. The technology was later enhanced by M. George Craford, also at General Electric, who improved the brightness and efficiency of red and yellow LEDs in 1972. The invention of the blue LED was a critical advancement made by Shuji Nakamura at Japanese chemical manufacturer Nichia Corporation in 1993, along with scientists Isamu Akasaki and Hiroshi Amano, who collaborated closely at Nagoya University.

Today, ICs power our computers, fibre optics and lasers facilitate the internet, and LEDs provide the display technology for almost all digital screens. Nobel Prizes in Physics were awarded to Marconi in 1909, Bardeen, Brattain and Shockley in 1956, Schawlow and Townes in 1964, Kilby in 2000, Kao in 2009, and Akasaki, Amano and Nakamura in 2014.

These technological developments did not enrich the businesses that sponsored them alone but also contributed to the development of the broader industry and beyond, with the development of one technology at one institution spurring the development of another, as the vacuum tube to transistor to IC development shows. However, the industry alone cannot innovate.

Businesses in countries such as the US, the UK and Japan have been R&D pioneers because they have a strong publicly funded research ecosystem, including universities and government laboratories. If 11 per cent of all Nobel-winning Physics discoveries happened at for-profit enterprises, the remaining 89 per cent have occurred at universities, government research laboratories and non-profit institutions.

The development of computing technology, including early vacuum tube systems, was significantly influenced by governmental efforts during the World Wars. For example, during World War II, Cambridge mathematician Alan Turing led efforts at Bletchley Park to decrypt messages encoded by the German Enigma machine. This period marked an accelerated arms race in computer technological development—for example, the British creation of the Colossus, the American development of the ENIAC and UNIVAC, and the German series of computers, Z1, Z2 and Z3.

As the Cold War unfolded, the 1950s witnessed rapid advancements in miniature electronics, driven by the space race and increasing demands in military and aerospace applications. The transistor, invented at Bell Labs in 1947, received significant funding from the US Department of Defence. The space race between the United States and the Soviet Union, especially during the moon missions, led to further developments in microchips and integrated circuits at companies like Texas Instruments, Fairchild Semiconductor and Intel. As much as $267 billion was spent on NASA's Apollo Moon Mission, benefiting several industries and universities.

These advancements often occurred in university-led clusters such as the Harvard–MIT cluster around Boston, the Stanford–Berkeley cluster around San Francisco (today called the Silicon Valley), and the UK's Golden Triangle cluster (Oxford, Cambridge and London). These provided a rich catchment of talent and conducted fundamental research essential for applied technological developments. They were also crucial in the development of the internet. Key university nodes in the early internet included UCLA, Stanford, MIT and University College London.

The development of the World Wide Web by Tim Berners-Lee at the European research organisation CERN occurred later, in the late 1980s and early 1990s. This innovation was instrumental in making the internet globally accessible, with the World Wide Web Consortium (W3C) later forming to develop web protocols for broad adoption.

Twentieth-century advances in fibre optics, lasers, and LEDs were also supported by various government agencies such as the U.S. Department of Defence and the Department of Energy. Notable academic contributions came from University College London, where Charles Kao developed foundational research in fibre optics, and Nagoya University, where Isamu Akasaki and Hiroshi Amano worked on developing the blue LED in collaboration with industry.

Artificial intelligence today also is a result of a confluence of government, industry and academia coming together, with research giants like Bell Labs, IBM, Google, Microsoft and Tesla, start-ups like DeepMind and OpenAI, universities like Stanford, MIT and Carnegie Mellon, and publicly funded institutions like the US National Science Foundation (NSF), EU Horizon grant, China's Next Generation AI Plan playing a critical role.

The 2024 Nobel Prize and DeepMind

The 2024 Nobel Prize in Chemistry was won by David Baker, Demis Hassabis and John Jumper for their work on computational protein structure design (Baker) and prediction (Hassabis and Jumper). The Nobel-winning technology AlphaFold, for which Hassabis and Jumper won part of the award, was developed by them at the London-based start-up DeepMind, of which Hassabis is the co-founder.

A robust innovation ecosystem requires both for-profit and non-profits to work together. All of these are necessary: a government that supports the funding of foundational as well as capital-intensive research (as during the space race) and a university system that conducts foundational research such as development in material science, theoretical physics and computer science, while also creating a large pool of skilled scientists who work across academia, government and industry to spearhead research. Finally, a thriving and competitive business environment enables businesses to spearhead applied innovations. Hence, innovation creates public goods, and businesses can contribute to and benefit from an innovative ecosystem.

Reaching the Last Mile

Nobel-worthy technologies expand the human frontier, and such frontier expansion has been at the heart of economic growth and creative destruction. In different periods, different industries have driven this expansion: steelmaking and the railways in the nineteenth century driven by coal, the automotive revolution in the early twentieth century driven by oil, electronics and communication in the late twentieth century and the ICT revolution today driven by electricity, the ongoing AI and biotechnology revolutions, and the renewable revolution in energy.

Historically, select innovation clusters have been at the frontier of economic growth. From ancient Asian cities like Pataliputra (until the sixth century) and Baghdad (from the ninth to the twelfth century) to European cities like Florence, Paris, London, Oxford, Cambridge, Amsterdam, Berlin and Vienna, to American frontiers like Boston, Chicago and San Francisco and East Asian hubs like Tokyo and Seoul, to new emerging centres like Tel Aviv, Taipei, Shenzhen, and Bangalore, the frontier has kept moving, but has been clustered. This is because the coming together of talented individuals and capital at a focused location has agglomeration advantages. Businesses in such cities have unique opportunities for contributing to the human frontier.

Another frontier exists—that of reaching the last mile. If sending the first human to Mars is a challenge of frontier technology, making the benefits of progress reach every human being and our flora and fauna is the challenge of reaching the last mile. Just like the capability for innovation, especially applied innovation, businesses also have the unique capability of orchestrating and participating in deep supply chains.

Supply chains are the lifeline of the global economy. Since the dawn of civilisation, trade routes such as the ancient land Silk

Route or the Indian Ocean sea route made sure that commodities and innovations from one part of the world reached another. Businesses (traders) are the central players of such supply chains.

When supply chains get disrupted, it has major implications for the global world order. For example, when the land route connecting Europe and Asia through Constantinople (now called Istanbul, Türkiye) was disrupted with the Fall of Constantinople in 1453 at the hands of the Ottoman Empire, it heralded the Age of Exploration, during which Europeans began to look for alternate sea routes to Asia through the Atlantic Ocean.

Similarly, poor supply chains can make powerful nations kneel in wars. In 1941 during World War II, powerful and dominant Germany faced a deadly blow at the hands of the Soviet Union when, during the harsh winter, they failed to procure enough supplies of food, clothing and equipment for their soldiers at the frontier just a few miles away from Moscow, the Soviet capital. Logistics played spoilsport for Adolf Hitler, whose murderous Nazi regime otherwise seemed invincible.

With its large and diverse geography and dense yet highly remote corners, India offers unique logistical challenges, which businesses, especially in the fast-moving consumer goods (FMCG) industry, have overcome with their adept supply chain-building practices. For example, small packets of Maggi noodles, a Swiss instant food prepared, sold and distributed by food giant Nestle, can be found in the remotest corners of India, including high up in the Himalayan mountains. Another Nestle product, Nescafe, a staple for Allied soldiers in World War II, can also be found across India. The same applies to Frito Lay chips and a Pepsi cola bottle, available at roadside stalls across India.

The Indian conglomerate Indian Tobacco Company (ITC) turned its deep supply chain capabilities supplying tobacco products (cigarettes) to paan shops across India into a multibillion-dollar FMCG business in the 2000s, today becoming India's second largest FMCG brand with household names like Aashirvaad (packaged flour), Sunfeast (biscuits, bakery and noodles) and Bingo (chips). Similarly, household Indian brands like Parle and Britannia and their various products (Parle G biscuit or Britannia cakes) are household names in places where even cars do not reach.

These supply chains comprise a vast network of country-wide small and big private distributors who procure products from these brands and sell them to a wider network of mom-and-pop (*kirana*) shops. The massive sector employs an estimated 8 per cent of India's population. Several modern, sophisticated and more centralised Walmart-like retail chains have tried developing a presence in India.[85] However, organised retail only makes up 12 per cent of the country's retail sector and is primarily present in India's larger cities. The remaining 88 per cent remains unorganised, and their economic dominance is not expected to erode any time soon, given the complexity of Indian logistics. Supply chains in regions like the Himalayas or the forests of the Chotanagpur plateau require a more distributive approach to retail and supply chain, which local distributors and retailers excel at, as they know the local conditions through long-nurtured relationships far better than a retail giant, regardless of the giant's analytical sophistication.

These supply chain networks extend downstream from the business to the customer and go through the entire value chain, from farmer to customer, with businesses as the intermediaries. Businesses can be catalysts for positive change as the central orchestrators in these supply chains. They can push better labour and environmental standards in their upstream supply chains just as farmer-oriented businesses like ITC (and its e-Chaupaal agricultural initiative), Starbucks and Unilever have attempted to.

Iodised Salt

Businesses can push for goods and services that create large positive externalities for their customers downstream. The iodisation of salt consumed in households presents one such business innovation that has led to large positive externalities. In the early 1900s, iodine deficiency was a major health concern worldwide, leading to diseases like goitre. In 1924, the Morton Salt Company began selling iodised salt in the United States. With greater awareness, Americans began to buy iodised salt over non-iodised salt, which cost the same but had significant benefits. Iodine deficiency and the prevalence of goitre have reduced since the introduction of iodised salt. A 2017 study found that introducing iodised salt in 2024 also raised the IQ of those most deficient in iodine.[86]

The procurement and distribution capabilities of businesses can also become very valuable in times of crisis.[87] During the first wave of the COVID-19 pandemic, when India underwent a stringent lockdown in March 2020, Indian conglomerate Mahindra offered its automobile production plants to develop low-cost ventilators. Furthermore, FMCG businesses collaborated with industry bodies and government agencies to facilitate the movement and distribution of essential items across India despite the stringent lockdown measures. E-commerce giants like Amazon and Flipkart transformed their operations to focus on essential supplies, significantly ramping up their capabilities to meet the increased demand for essential and medical supplies.

When businesses deploy their capabilities to innovate and organise for public good, they can be one of the most transformational forces for prosperity and progress, expanding the human frontier.

20

Bring the Community Together with a Vision

Organisations can leave a positive legacy by uniting their own and stakeholder capabilities with a vision.

WHILE businesses have unique capabilities necessary for producing large public goods like breakthrough innovations and deep-reaching logistics, they are not sufficient.[88] For example, managing the COVID-19 pandemic required coordination between governments, NGOs and for-profit businesses, as each organisational form had unique capabilities. Although AstraZeneca had good drug development capabilities, it was not able to reach populations to the last mile. It needed the help of other businesses, like the Serum Institute (for manufacturing), governments and NGOs to get the job done.

While for-profit businesses are good at innovation, manufacturing and logistics capabilities, when it comes to other capabilities like last-mile delivery and coordination, other organisational forms have a greater advantage. For example, the large-scale coordination of vaccination was possible only because of the proactive role played by national and state governments, which naturally excel at coordination capabilities, which businesses can (at best) only moderately do. One of the reasons why governments tend to have better coordination abilities is because they can use their administrative power to 'order' the marshalling of resources for missions that require multiple stakeholders. This is why the army is often the best organisation to handle emergencies and natural disasters, as they can coordinate stakeholders and resources like no other.

Similarly, reaching the last mile is often better done by NGOs, which have significantly better capabilities in local management and grassroots collective action than private businesses or governments. While businesses and governments can reach the villages and streets, NGOs that include political organisations are better positioned to reach each household through their grassroots engagement and relationships. This is why, during the COVID-19 pandemic, NGOs were necessary to ensure their resources reached the right persons in need.

The 2020 Indian Migrant Crisis

The pandemic triggered a migrant crisis in India,[89] where the plight of migrants working in jobs such as construction and hospitality was ignored, leading to a large-scale return of migrants to their hometowns, leaving many stranded. One of the reasons governments, businesses and even local NGOs failed to address their needs was because very few organisations served low-income migrants, as most focused on the welfare of locals, making these migrants, who form the backbone of most urban economies, invisible.

When businesses try to develop commons, they should actively engage with stakeholders to identify unique capabilities they can bring to the table and how they can be leveraged. Various stakeholders are needed in all stages of strategic decision-making—producing goods and services, competing in markets, understanding externalities and generating commons.

Organisation type	Key capability	Why?	Example
Government	**Coordination** for aligning response efforts across sectors	Government has access to the entirety of state machinery, at different levels.	State and central governments coordinated the tracing and tracking of potential COVID-infected patients.
Non-profits	**Local governance** for adapting policies to local needs.	Non-profits are well connected at the grassroots and good at ensuring the last mile / person delivery.	An NGO named SWAN emerged to help stranded migrant workers with essential supplies.

Organisation type	Key capability	Why?	Example
Businesses	**Procurement, manufacturing and distribution** for the availability of essential goods across regions	Businesses have deep supplier networks, design and development capabilities, production facilities, and logistical capabilities.	Mahindra tied up with BEL and BHEL to design and scale up production of ventilators and Ambu bags. Amazon used its logistics capabilities to deliver not just food items to consumers, but also PPEs to doctors and hospitals.

How can managers bring them all together? A clear and consistent vision is necessary. Vision documents play an indispensable role in stakeholder management, as they are the most critical way a business can signal its long-term direction and provide guidance to all stakeholders about the direction they must follow.

These days, organisations tend to have vision statements, but very few are ever taken seriously. In such cases, they cease to be strategic documents. For a vision document to be strategically significant, it must provide a clear and not a vague signal of the direction of the business. It should also be viewed as a credible statement by the stakeholders. Given the strategic value vision documents can have, they must be designed participatively (using a design thinking process), so that they are viewed credibly by different stakeholders.

When vision documents are taken seriously, they can raise entire ecosystems. The 1960s US Lunar Mission is an instance in history where the vision to reach the moon brought several industries and the government together to make technological leaps in various fields. Several legendary leaders, from Jamsetji Tata to Steve Jobs, also exhibit this ability to bring different stakeholders together with inspirational vision. In the end, leadership is this—the ability to have an aspirational vision and then leverage the capabilities of many towards the vision.

Your Vision for the New World

What vision can we, especially as leaders of the modern world, rally together for? The most effective way businesses can contribute to society is by asking this: *How can we use our resources to create product and process innovations that contribute to solving a great challenge of our times?* If you are a leader, you can ask, how can my organisation help solve one tiny part of the world's more significant challenges? Can we help advance medical science like DeepMind did with AlphaFold? Can we develop sustainable supply chains like Unilever is trying to do? Can we accelerate the societal switch to green technologies, as Tata hopes to do for India? Can we create technologies that foster inclusion, as Apple does for people with special needs? Can we help enhance access to education, as Google does through its various free services? How can our *core* product and processes create innovations that serve the broader good?

As we have discussed several times, asking this question requires us to take stock of our core capabilities as well as our stakeholders'.

Can we build an ecosystem with stakeholders that consistently generates innovations for the public good? At the same time, we must undertake atypical testing by constantly reaching out to atypical stakeholders, asking *how we can identify and minimise our negative footprint in the world.*

This century is not one of individual titans and stalwarts. Our challenges today are too complex to be solved alone. We need to work with each other, raising an ecosystem that leaves a positive footprint in the world. We can only do that through a *mindset of grounded leadership* and a *willingness to listen to different stakeholders with empathy* so that we solve the right problems and follow an impeccable code of conduct that nurtures long-term relationships built on trust.

A vision is the final statement that credibly brings the intentions and capabilities of our stakeholders together. Consider Jamsetji's vision for Tata, which has lasted for nearly two centuries and has shaped the direction of the conglomerate he founded. One of Tatas' first and most pioneering achievements was building Jamshedpur in the middle of the dense forest, which was not just India's steel plant but the door through which India entered the twentieth century. Central to Tata's vision was a township with 'wide streets', 'shady trees', 'lawns and gardens', 'football, hockey and parks' and 'temples, ... mosques and ... churches'; a place that not only cared about profits but also about welfare, not just of the employees but their families and beyond.

To propel our current world, we need many new Jamshedpurs—communities that create wealth for the economy and leave a positive footprint in the lives of people around: a community where everyone, including nature, is a little wealthier. As Tata's erstwhile chairman J.R.D Tata wrote about the purpose of wealth, 'The whole of that wealth is held in trust for the people and used exclusively for their benefit. The cycle is thus complete; what came from the people has gone back to the people many times over.'[90]

~~Win~~ ***Nurture*:**

- Free enterprise rests on public goods, and public goods rest on a sense of community.
- The modern corporation with its narrow shareholder focus may not survive the new world.
- A future may be businesses owned by charities; they have a history of commercial success and social good.
- From scientific innovation to last-mile connectivity, there are many ways businesses can create commons.
- Organisations can leave a positive legacy by uniting their own and stakeholder capabilities with a vision.

Conclusion

We have now explored five essential rules of strategy that are urgently needed for the challenges of the modern world. Our challenges are atypical, inviting us to be far more conscious about the footprint of our actions than before. So, we also need new rules that may seem atypical to solve them.

Rule 0: ***Value*** **~~intellect~~** ***empathy***, a more crucial skill than ever in a world where AI can automate tasks like data analysis and coding. In a world where leaders lack empathy, crises emerge as stakeholders at the fringes are systematically ignored. Data cannot substitute empathy, as the data generation process is slow and biased by power. So, the ability to listen to the stories of others is an essential skill for motivating action. Applying design thinking in strategy that prioritises empathy and listening can help us understand systems better and create resilient organisations.

Rule 1: ***Lead from the*** **~~top~~** ***ground***, so leadership is grounded in the people, always listening to those who toil to get things done. Successful organisations have inimitable capabilities embedded in their relational contracts and trust between different stakeholders. Nurturing this trust takes time and commitment, but once developed, it is immensely valuable and challenging for others to replicate, especially in an era where business has become more transactional. Successful organisations hone leadership at every level of the organisation, which gets difficult and complex tasks done that no individual 'boss' can direct.

Rule 2: ***Pursue*** **~~profit~~** ***innovation*** and not dirty strategies that create pollution, opaqueness and barriers for others to enter. Dirty strategies make organisations vulnerable in the long run, as they become targets of market and non-market stakeholders and regulators. In the long run, the only good strategy tends to be innovation—either in products or processes. An organisation's long-term goal must be to nurture innovative ecosystems that can survive and even thrive in the face of creative destruction.

Rule 3: ***Hear the*** **~~typicals~~** ***atypicals***. All businesses have some invisible negative externalities that atypical voices at the fringes often know first. Good organisations do not ignore their core product. However, they also do not ignore such fringe voices and consistently put their products and processes through atypical testing, creating more resilient businesses.

Rule 4: **~~Win~~** ***Nurture commons***, which is essential for a sustainable and prosperous society. Good organisations nurture commons as their true legacy and do not have a narrow shareholder focus. Some good businesses, like the Tatas, are owned by charities, providing a potential roadmap for the future. Some of the commons socially conscious organisations can create are scientific innovation and providing last mile connectivity. For-profit businesses bring many unique capabilities to society, such as production and distribution abilities. Good organisations leverage these capabilities, working with other stakeholders to leave a positive legacy.

These five rules of strategy in this book are a call to action to remind us that we are, above all else, citizens of the only planet we know as home. We are all humans first. Our roles as managers of our organisations come second.

In this context, the advice of Nobel Laureate Toni Morrison to her students is very pertinent, 'I tell my students, "When you get these jobs that you have been so brilliantly trained for, just remember that your real job is that if you are free, you need to free somebody else. If you have some power, then your job is to empower somebody else. This is not just a grab-bag candy game."'[91]

I would end this book with Morrison's words, just as I started. The world is not a grab-bag candy game. It does not need to be a tournament with trophies for a few and uncertainty and insecurity for the rest. The modern world and its challenges afford us no place for such a skewed society of haves and have-nots.

None of us can create a positive impact alone. Even the Buddha created a sangha. Our true joy and legacy lie in nurturing organisations that create a more free and empowered world. A more empathetic world, with grounded and innovative leaders—you, the reader—who listen to everyone and create commons for the benefit of all as their legacy.

Notes

Introduction

1 Wells, H.G. (1918). *In the Fourth Year: Anticipations of a World Peace.* Chatto & Windus.
2 Gandhi, M.K. (1928). 'Capitalists Of India'. *Young India.*
3 Raj, P., & Richter, B.K. (2021). 'Corporate Market Stewardship'. Working Paper.

Rule 0: VALUE ~~INTELLECT~~ EMPATHY

I. Learning from the Fringes

1 Commonly attributed to the Dalai Lama.
2 HK01. (2020). '[Wuhan Pneumonia] Guan Yi: The source of the disease has been destroyed and experts are not welcome. The scale of infection is estimated to be ten times that of SARS'. *HK01,* January 23. https://www.hk01.com/社會新聞/425644/武漢肺炎-管軼-病源被毀-不歡迎專家-估感染規模大沙士十倍.
3 World Health Organisation. (2020). [Post on X]. X, January 14. https://x.com/WHO/status/1217043229427761152?lang=en.
4 Shapira, R., & Zingales, L. (2017). 'Is pollution value-maximizing? The DuPont Case'. *National Bureau of Economic Research.*

5 Gounaridis, D., & Newell, J. P. (2024). 'The social anatomy of climate change denial in the United States'. *Scientific Reports, 14(1), 2097.*
6 HK01, 2020.
7 Wiesel, E. (1960). Night. Bantam Books.
8 Angelou, M. (1978). *And Still I Rise.* Random House.

II. Intelligence in the Age of AI

9 Searle, J. (1980). 'Minds, brains and programs'. *Behavioral and Brain Sciences, 3(3),* 417–424.
10 Roots of Empathy. (2019). https://rootsofempathy.org/wp-content/uploads/2022/04/Roots-of-Empathy-Full-Research-Summary-2021.pdf.

III. Strategic Design Thinking

11 IDEO U. *Design Thinking.* https://www.ideou.com/pages/design-thinking.
12 The strategic design thinking process was initially developed jointly with Vikram Kohli, SPA Bhopal, as part of the design methodology module of the Strategic Stewardship course in September 2022.
13 There is no single method for identifying key emerging themes. A good principle, however, is to involve a variety of stakeholders to look at these stakeholder maps and identify emergent themes. Machine learning techniques like topic modelling may also come in handy if the data is large.

Rule 1: LEAD FROM THE ~~TOP~~ GROUND

Chapter 1: Strategy 101: Inimitable Capabilities

14 Shimokawa, K. (2012). *The Birth of Lean.* Lean Enterprise Institute.
15 This section presents a summarised version of my public lecture notes on IIM Bangalore's MBA core course *Competition and*

Strategy that I co-taught between 2018 and 2022, along with colleagues in IIMB's Strategy area.

16 Porter, M.E. (2008). 'The five competitive forces that shape strategy'. *Harvard Business Review, 86(1)*, 78.

Chapter 2: Capabilities Lie in Relationships

17 Magee, D. (2008). *How Toyota Became #1: Leadership Lessons from the World's Greatest Car Company.* Penguin Books India.

18 Schwantes, M. (2024). 'This 32-year-old Steve Jobs quote may be his best leadership lesson'. *Inc,* October 11. https://www.inc.com/marcel-schwantes/this-32-year-old-steve-jobs-quote-may-be-his-best-leadership-lesson-ever/90986760.

19 Guglielmo, C. (2013). 'Apple's Cook says "magic" happens when team players who aren't "political," don't crave recognition'. *Forbes*, June 4. https://www.forbes.com/sites/connieguglielmo/2013/06/04/apples-cook-says-magic-happens-with-team-players-who-arent-political-dont-crave-recognition/.

Chapter 3: Nurturing Trust in Organisations

20 I benefitted greatly from the books *The Tatas: How a Family Built a Business and a Nation* by Girish Kuber (HarperCollins, 2019) *and Tata: The Global Corporation that Built Indian Capitalism* by Mircea Raianu (Harvard University Press, 2021), and from the 'About our Heritage' section of the website tata.com.

21 Tata Sons. *About Us.* https://www.tata.com/business/tata-sons.

22 Masani, Z., & Venema, V. (2015). 'Men of steel with a softer side'. *BBC News,* February 3. https://www.bbc.com/news/magazine-31057308.

23 Lala, R.M. (2004). *The Creation of Wealth: The Tatas from the 19th to the 21st Century.* Penguin Books India.

24 Tata Trusts. *Jamsetji N. Tata's Vision for India.* https://www.tatatrusts.org/about-tatatrusts/jamsetji-n-tata.

25 Khanna, T., & Yafeh, Y. (2007). 'Business groups in emerging markets: Paragons or parasites?'. *Journal of Economic Literature, 45(2)*, 331–372.

26 *The Times of India.* (2024). 'The tall leader: When Ratan Tata stood outside Taj Hotel for 3 days during 26/11 Mumbai terror attack'. *The Times of India,* October 10. https://timesofindia.indiatimes.com/india/the-tall-leader-when-ratan-tata-stood-outside-taj-hotel-for-3-days-during-26/11-mumbai-terror-attack/articleshow/114119884.cms.

Chapter 5: Leading with a Himalayan Mindset

27 Tripathi, P.S., & Ramakrishnan, V. (2020). 'Beware of the "Yes Man"'. *Frontline,* June 18. https://frontline.thehindu.com/the-nation/beware-the-yes-man/article31765890.ece.

28 Manekshaw, S. (2001). 'Leadership in the 21st century'. In K.M. Field Marshal (Ed.), *Cariappa: Memorial Lectures 1995-2000.*

29 Aghion, P., Bloom, N., Lucking, B., Sadun, R., & Van Reenen, J. (2021). 'Turbulence, firm decentralization, and growth in bad times'. *American Economic Journal: Applied Economics, 13(1),* 133–169.

30 A version of this section appeared as a 2016 article 'How to come up with a strategy under true uncertainty' in the *LSE Business Review.*

31 Saxenian, A. (1996). *Regional Advantage: Culture and Competition in Silicon Valley and Route 128.* Harvard University Press.

32 Schwantes, M. (2018). 'A young Steve Jobs once gave this priceless leadership lesson'. *Inc,* March 28. https://www.inc.com/marcel-schwantes/a-young-steve-jobs-once-gave-this-priceless-leadership-lesson-here-it-is-in-a-few-sentences.html.

33 A description of the Himalayan Mindset first appeared in 2001 in *Hindu Business Line On Campus,* as an article titled 'What the trek to a Himalayan peak taught me'. https://www.iimb.ac.in/sites/default/files/2020-01/What-trek-Himalayan-peak.pdf.

34 The origin of this quote is disputed. *Quote Investigator.* https://quoteinvestigator.com/2016/08/18/conquer/.

35 Amabile, T., & Kramer, S. (2011). *The Progress Principle: Using Small Wins to Ignite Joy, Engagement, and Creativity at Work.* Harvard Business Press.

Rule 2: PURSUE ~~PROFIT~~ INNOVATION

Chapter 6: Dirty Strategies

36 Schumpeter, J.A. (1942). *Capitalism, Socialism and Democracy.* Harper & Brothers.
37 Shapira and Zingales, 2017.
38 United States Environmental Protection Agency. (2006). '100 percent participation and commitment in EPA's PFOA Stewardship Program'. *EPA Newsroom Archive,* March 2. https://www.epa.gov/archive/epapages/newsroom_archive/newsreleases/95de36c6115a523a8525712500693772.html.
39 McMullen, J. (2022). 'The audacious PR plot that seeded doubt about climate change'. *BBC News,* July 23. https://www.bbc.com/news/science-environment-62225696.
40 Fontanella-Khan, J. (2013). 'Brussels: Astroturfing takes root'. *Financial Times,* June 26. https://www.ft.com/content/74271926-dd9f-11e2-a756-00144feab7de.

Chapter 7: Self-correcting Markets

41 Swift, T. (2014). 'For Taylor Swift, the future of music is a love story'. *Wall Street Journal,* July 27. https://www.wsj.com/articles/for-taylor-swift-the-future-of-music-is-a-love-story-1404763219.

Chapter 8: The Role of Regulators

42 Singh, S., & Kaushik, K. (2018). 'Videocon gets Rs 3250-crore loan from ICICI Bank, bank CEO's husband gets sweet deal from Venugopal Dhoot'. *The Indian Express*, March 29. https://indianexpress.com/article/express-exclusive/videocon-gets-rs-3250-cr-loan-from-icici-bank-chanda-kochhars-husband-gets-sweet-deal-from-venugopal-dhoot-5115267/.
43 Jagannath, J. (2022). 'Meet Arvind Gupta! The whistleblower responsible for Chanda Kochhar, Venugopal Dhoot's arrests'. *Business Today,* December 29. https://www.businesstoday.in/latest/corporate/story/meet-arvind-gupta-the-whistleblower-responsible-for-chanda-kochhar-venugopal-dhoots-arrests-358194-2022-12-29.

Chapter 9: Good Strategies Innovate

44 *Reuters*. (2024). 'Apple supplier Foxconn said to reject married women from India iPhone jobs'. *The Hindu,* June 26. https://www.thehindu.com/business/Industry/apple-supplier-foxconn-said-to-reject-married-women-from-india-iphone-jobs/article68336276.ece.

45 Bajarin, T. (2017). 'How Corning's crash project for Steve Jobs helped define the iPhone'. *Fast Company,* November 10. https://www.fastcompany.com/40493737/how-cornings-crash-project-for-steve-jobs-helped-define-the-iphone.

Chapter 10: Know Your Village for Creative Destruction

46 Mihm, S. (2022). 'Mass layoffs in big tech are an old-guard mistake'. *Bloomberg,* November 15. https://www.bloomberg.com/opinion/articles/2022-11-15/mass-layoffs-at-twitter-meta-amazon-an-old-guard-mistake?embedded-checkout=true.

47 Sucher, S.J., & Westner, M.M. (2022). 'What companies still get wrong about layoffs'. *Harvard Business Review*, December 8. https://hbr.org/2022/12/what-companies-still-get-wrong-about-layoffs.

Rule 3: HEAR THE ~~TYPICALS~~ ATYPICALS

Chapter 11: Design Isn't Neutral

48 Obermeyer, Z., Powers, B., Vogeli, C., & Mullainathan, S. (2019). 'Dissecting racial bias in an algorithm used to manage the health of populations'. *Science, 366(6464),* 447–453.

49 Shapira & Zingales, 2017.

Chapter 12: Products Have Externalities

50 Subramanian, T.S. (2018). 'Wastelands of the Noyyal'. *Frontline,* January 31. https://frontline.thehindu.com/the-nation/wastelands-of-the-noyyal/article10055526.ece.

51 Press Release. (2013). 'Generic drug manufacturer Ranbaxy pleads guilty and agrees to pay $500 million to resolve false

claims allegations, cGMP violations and false statements to the FDA'. *U.S. Department of Justice*, May 13. https://www.justice.gov/opa/pr/generic-drug-manufacturer-ranbaxy-pleads-guilty-and-agrees-pay-500-million-resolve-false.

52 Haidt, J. (2024). *The Anxious Generation: How the Great Rewiring of Childhood is Causing an Epidemic of Mental Illness.* Random House.

53 Zuboff, S. (2018). *The Age of Surveillance Capitalism: The Fight for a Human Future at the New Frontier of Power.* Profile Books.

Chapter 13: Atypical Stakeholders Know First

54 TOI Lifestyle Desk. (2024). 'What's driving cancer rate in Malwa, the cotton belt of the country?'. *The Times of India*, March 10. https://timesofindia.indiatimes.com/life-style/health-fitness/health-news/whats-driving-cancer-rate-in-malwa-the-cotton-belt-of-the-country/articleshow/108362171.cms.

55 Human Rights Watch. (2018). 'Hidden Chains: Rights Abuses and Forced Labor in Thailand's Fishing Industry', January 23. https://www.hrw.org/report/2018/01/23/hidden-chains/rights-abuses-and-forced-labor-thailands-fishing-industry#_ftn4.

56 *Amnesty International*. (2023). 'The Gambia: Devastating impact of overfishing on local communities.' *Amnesty International*, May 31. https://www.amnesty.org/en/latest/news/2023/05/the-gambia-devastating-impact-of-overfishing-on-local-communities/.

57 Koundal, A. (2023). 'Solar power should not come at the cost of locals' land: Sonam Wangchuk'. *The Economic Times*, February 17. https://energy.economictimes.indiatimes.com/news/renewable/solar-power-should-not-come-at-the-cost-of-locals-land-sonam-wangchuk/97985643.

58 *The Times of India*. (2023). 'Ujjain teen dies by suicide; was bullied online for wearing makeup.' *The Times of India*, November 26. https://timesofindia.indiatimes.com/etimes/trending/tragic-death-of-ujjain-teen-priyanshu-yadav-due-to-online-bullying/articleshow/105511796.cms.

59 Camuffo, A., Cordova, A., Gambardella, A., & Spina, C. (2020). 'A scientific approach to entrepreneurial decision-making: Evidence from a randomized control trial'. *Management Science, 66(2)*, 564–586.

60 Baer, D. (2014). 'Mark Zuckerberg explains why Facebook doesn't "move fast and break things" anymore'. *Business Insider,* May 3. https://www.businessinsider.in/strategy/mark-zuckerberg-explains-why-facebook-doesnt-move-fast-and-break-things-anymore/articleshow/34555538.cms.

Chapter 14: Moral and Amoral Drift

61 Sheera, F., and Conger, K. (2022). 'Hate Speech's Rise on Twitter Is Unprecedented, Researchers Find'. *The New York Times,* 2 December. https://www.nytimes.com/2022/12/02/technology/twitter-hate-speech.html

62 Hart, O. & Zingales, L. (2017). 'Companies Should Maximize Shareholder Welfare Not Market Value'. *Journal of Law, Finance, and Accounting, 2(2)*, 247–275.

63 Dang, S. (2023). 'US ad revenue at Musk's X declined each month since takeover: Data'. *Reuters,* October 5. https://www.reuters.com/technology/us-ad-revenue-musks-x-declined-each-month-since-takeover-data-2023-10-04/.

64 Ingram, D. (2024). 'Fewer people are using Elon Musk's X as the platform struggles to attract and keep users, according to analysts'. *NBC News,* March 23. https://www.nbcnews.com/tech/tech-news/fewer-people-using-elon-musks-x-struggles-keep-users-rcna144115.

65 Morris, C. (2024). 'X is now worth less than 25% of what Elon Musk paid for it'. *Fortune*, September 30. https://fortune.com/2024/09/30/x-value-drops-fidelity-investment-elon-musk-twitter-buyout/.

66 Kihara L. (2022). 'Elon Musk says "I have too much work on my plate"'. *Reuters*, November 14. https://www.reuters.com/technology/elon-musk-says-i-have-too-much-work-my-plate-2022-11-14/.

Chapter 15: Embracing Atypical Testing

67 WSJ Staff. (2010). 'Buffett's 1991 Salomon Testimony'. *The Wall Street Journal*, May 1. https://www.wsj.com/articles/BL-MB-21380.

68 Shapira & Zingales, 2017.

Rule 4: ~~WIN~~ NURTURE

Chapter 16: Public Goods Capitalism

69 *The Economic Times*. (2024). 'Just 6 words: How Ratan Tata wanted to be remembered after his death'. *The Economic Times,* October 14. https://economictimes.indiatimes.com/magazines/panache/how-ratan-tata-wanted-to-be-remembered-in-6-words-only/articleshow/114190669.cms?from=mdr.

70 This section borrows from my public lecture notes on the multi-level course *Evolution of Business and Markets*, which I have taught at IIMB since 2018.

71 Rajan, R.G., & Zingales, L. (2009). 'Which Capitalism? Lessons from the East Asian Crisis'. *Global Corporate Governance* (135–148). Columbia University Press.

72 Lucas, R.E. (2018). 'What was the industrial revolution?'. *Journal of Human Capital, 12(2)*, 182–203.

73 Mokyr, J. (2016). *A Culture of Growth: The Origins of the Modern Economy.* Princeton University Press.

74 Public goods and commons can be operated by private players—where the public hands over the operations of a publicly funded hospital, road or a mine to a private player for a set period of time, if it is hoped that it can operate the hospital more efficiently, while the access to good remains freely (or at nominal rates) open to all.

Chapter 17: The Future of Business

75 Meier, B. (2018). 'Origins of an Epidemic: Purdue Pharma Knew Its Opioids Were Widely Abused'. *The New York Times,* 29 May. https://www.nytimes.com/2018/05/29/health/purdue-opioids-oxycontin.html.

76 Marks, J.H. (2020). 'Lessons from corporate influence in the opioid epidemic: Toward a norm of separation'. *Journal of Bioethical Inquiry, 17,* 173–189.

77 Lamarre, E., Mansour, T., & Tetrault, J. (2012). 'McKinsey on cooperatives'. *McKinsey.*

Chapter 18: Philanthropy-owned Businesses

78 Some philanthropies such as the US-based Lilly Foundation and the Canada-based Mastercard Foundation hold minority ownership in businesses such as pharmaceutical giant Eli Lilly and payments card major Mastercard, respectively, having substantial, but not controlling, influence over their companies.

79 Thomsen, S., Poulsen, T., Børsting, C., & Kuhn, J. (2018). 'Industrial foundations as long-term owners'. *Corporate Governance: An International Review, 26(3),* 180–196.

80 Børsting, C., & Thomsen, S. (2017). 'Foundation ownership, reputation, and labour'. *Oxford Review of Economic Policy, 33(2),* 317–338.

81 Thomsen, S., & Rose, C. (2004). 'Foundation ownership and financial performance: Do companies need owners?'. *European Journal of Law and Economics,* 18, 343–364.

82 Thompson, G. (2018). 'Foundation ownership and firm performance: A review of the international evidence'. *Corporate Governance in Contention.*

83 Thompson, 2018.

Chapter 19: What Good Can Businesses Do?

84 Zhang, L., & Zhang, Q. (2023). 'Mapping the scientific and technological landscape: An analysis of Nobel Prize-producing institutions'. *Scientometrics, 128(11),* 6129–6145.

85 Yadav, R. (2024). 'Retail & E-commerce: Indian retail market is projected to reach $2 trillion by 2032'. *Invest India.* https://www.investindia.gov.in/sector/retail-e-commerce.

86 Feyrer, J., Politi, D., & Weil, D.N. (2017). 'The cognitive effects of micronutrient deficiency: Evidence from salt iodization in the United States'. *Journal of the European Economic Association, 15(2),* 355–387.

87 Saranga, H., & Raj, P. (2021). 'How to manage large-scale public crises'. *Stanford Social Innovation Review.*

88 This section draws from my 2021 research conducted with Haritha Saranga on handling large scale public crises, published in the *Stanford Social Innovation Review*.

Chapter 20: Bring the Community Together with a Vision

89 Bhalla, M., Raj, P., & Sastry, T. (2020). 'Why do migrants get such a raw deal?'. *The Hindu Business Line*, May 12. https://www.thehindubusinessline.com/opinion/why-do-migrants-get-such-a-raw-deal/article31559857.ece.

90 Gopalakrishnan, K., & Bhat, H. (2024). *Jamsetji Tata: Powerful Learnings for Corporate Success.* Penguin Random House India.

Conclusion

91 Morrison, T. (2003). 'The truest eye'. *O, The Oprah Magazine.* https://www.oprah.com/omagazine/Toni-Morrison-Talks-Love/4.

Index

Aashirvaad, 199
actionable points, 19–20
adenoviral vector technology, 95
advisory industry, 116, 123
Age of Exploration, 198
agrarian movements, 39
agriculture sector, externalities of, 113, 120, 125
airlines industry, 24
Akasaki, Isamu, 193, 195
AlphaFold, 195, 205
Altman, Sam, 76
Amano, Hiroshi, 193, 195
Amazon, 27, 68, 70, 200
Amazon rainforest, 114
Amnesty International reports, 126
amoral drift, 136–138, 187
Amsterdam, 157–158
Amul, 172, 178
Android mobile operating system, 25
anti-competitive 'dirty' strategies, 25
anti-privacy laws, 64
Antwerp, 157–158
Apple, 26, 28, 50, 52, 58, 69–70, 75, 90, 97, 205
  collaborative culture of innovation, 32–34
  in-app payment system, 69–70
  iOS mobile operating system, 25, 70, 76
  iPhone, 25, 90, 92–93, 97, 103, 110
  iTunes music service, 104
  walled-garden approach, 110
App Store, 110
App Tracking Transparency (ATT), 76
artificial intelligence (AI), 11, 26, 101, 195, 197
  power of, 10

asks, identifying, 17–18, 21
AstraZeneca, 96, 201
  vaccine, 95
astroturfing, 65
attractiveness bias, 14
attribution bias, 14
atypicals, 209
  impacts of, 125–128
  stakeholders, 130
atypical testing, 128–133, 142
  effective checks and balances, 148–151
  identify externalities, 144–146
  inviting diverse and critical guest list, 142–143
  transparency of products and processes, 146–148
automotive revolution, 197
average tenure, 92
Azim Premji Foundation, 183

Baker, David, 195–196
Ballmer, Steve, 179
banking and finance sectors, externalities of, 116, 122
Bardeen, John, 192
Battle of Plassey in 1757, 160
Bellary illegal mining, 113
Bell Labs, 191–195
Berkshire Hathaway, 173
Berners-Lee, Tim, 195
Bharat Biotech, 95–96
Bhopal Gas disaster, 1984, 6, 127
Bhopal Gas Tragedy, 1984, 115
Bilott, Robert, 4–5, 82
Bingo, 199
BioNTech, 95
Blackberry and Blackberry OS, 25
blind spot bias, 14
Blockbuster, 102–103
blueprint leadership, 51
boardroom leadership, 51
Bosch, 182, 186
Boston's Route 128, 51–52
Brattain, Walter, 192
Britannia, 199
British East India Company, 157
British Petroleum 2010 Deepwater Horizon oil spill, 114
Buffet, Warren, 144, 146
'burning cash' model, 67–68
Burroughs Wellcome, 189
businesses
  capital-owned, 178
  environment, early 2010s, 73–74
  labour-owned, 178
  as a production system, 178
business groups, 173, 176
buyers, 74–75, 78

capabilities of businesses, 26–29, 31, 89–91, 197, 201–202
  organisation type and, 203–204
  procurement and distribution, 200
capitalism
  free enterprise, 160
  history of, 156–160

medieval economy of Europe, 157–158
carbon emissions, 114, 116, 118, 126
Carlsberg, 182–183
Carl Zeiss, 182–193
caste system, 156
Catalent, 95–96
censorship, 123
Central Board of Film Certification, 86, 147
charismatic individuals, 52
chemical and radioactive waste, 114
chemical-intensive agriculture, externalities of, 125
chemicals industry, 114–115
chemicals industry, externalities of, 114, 122
Chernobyl nuclear disaster, 1986, 6
child labour ban, 99
Chinese manufacturing industries, 44, 90–91
'Chinese Room' example, 11
civic groups, 81
climate denialism, 6, 70
Coal India, 173
Coca-Cola Foundation, 187
cola industry, 71, 74, 78
collaborative culture of innovation, 32–34
commercial service industries, externalities of, 117, 124
Communist movement, 38
Competition Commission of India (CCI), 83, 86
competitive advantage, 90
competitors, 74, 76–77, 79
computer technological development, 194
conglomerates, 173, 177
construction sector, externalities of, 115, 122
consumer electronics, 114, 121
consumer electronics, externalities of, 114, 121
content delivery network (CDN) technology, 103
content moderation policies, 110
contractual infrastructure, 160–161
Cook, Tim, 33–34, 97
cooperatives and modern corporations, 178–179
Corning Incorporated, 96–97
Covaxin vaccine, 95
COVID-19 pandemic, 2–4, 200–201
  vaccine development during, 94–96
C8 poisoning, 4–6, 63, 80–83, 117
Craford, M. George, 193
creative destruction, 102–105
credit cards, 66, 71
customers, 74, 78

data, 208
  limitations, 5–7

proprietary, 7
decentralised organisations, 50–51
decision-makers in a business, 99–102
DeepMind, 26, 195, 205
Deepwater Horizon oil spill, 126
Denmark, 188
design, 108, 208
selective nature of, 109–110
strategy, 110–112
design thinking dashboard, 20
desires, identifying, 17–18, 21
Detroit, 39, 43–44
Dickens, Charles, ix
digital crimes, 116
digital economy, externalities of, 118
Digital Markets Act, 2022, 70
dirty strategies, 80–81, 83, 89, 134–135, 137–138, 180
'burning cash' model, 67–68
by food industry, 65
increasing opaqueness, 65–66
lobbying efforts to evade negative externalities, 63–65
misleading claims by real estate industry, 65–66
misleading labelling, 66
raising barriers to entry, 66–70
by US tobacco industry, 65
disruptions, 26, 77, 115
Dorabji, 37–38
Dow Chemical, 127
Dunning Kruger effect, 14
DuPont, 47, 62, 100, 127, 147–148
lobbying efforts of, 63–64, 70
Teflon poisoning, 4–6, 63–64, 80–83, 111–112, 114, 117
top-down organisational design, 109
Dutch East India Company, 157
dysfunctional village, 98

ecosystem (village) centric approach, 120
Edison, Thomas, 192
Editors Guild of India, 86
education sector, externalities of, 116, 123
Einstein, Albert, 193
Eisenhower matrix, 19–20
electronics manufacturing, in India, 92–93
Eli Lilly, 67
empathy, 11–14, 21, 208
cognitive, 12
compassionate, 12
emotional, 12
employee-owned companies, 172, 174
employees, 75–76, 78
and layoffs, 100–102
as stakeholder, 100
employee stock ownership plans (ESOPs), 179

employee turnover, 92
empowerment, 92
Empress Mills, 36
Encyclopédie, 162
energy and power generation industry, externalities of, 114, 121
engaged teams, 56
engagement-type organisations, 49–50
enterprise foundations, 187
  advantages, 187–188
  challenges, 189–190
  limitations, 188–189
  ownership arrangement, 182
  ownership structure, 182–183, 188–189
  passing the ownership of, 188–189
  reputation and social responsibility ratings, 188
environmental regulation, 127
Epic Games, 69–70
ethnographic approach, 13
European Privacy Association, 64–65
European Union, 25
  certification requirements for exporters, 75
  regulation of monopolistic practices, 70
evasive organisations, 49–50
evergreening, 66–67
externalities, 113, 119–124, 131, 137–138, 142, 144, 146–148, 150
  identification of, 119–120, 144–146
  influence of, 146
  invisible nature of, 117–124
  monetary consequences of, 148–149
  negative, 63, 73, 81, 84, 87, 100, 129, 136–137, 180, 191, 209
  of plastics, 117–118
  positive, 200
  of products, 113–117, 151
  stakeholder engagement in decision-making, 150–151

Facebook, 76–77, 103
Fairchild Semiconductor, 192, 194
fairness, 102
fake news, 118
Fall of Constantinople in 1453, 198
family-controlled businesses, 173, 176
fast-moving consumer goods (FMCG), 198–199
Fenty Beauty, 111
financial crisis, 2008, 149
Fisher, Ronald, 117
Fleming, John Ambrose, 192
Flint water crisis, 2014, 115
Flipkart, 85–86, 200
food and beverage industry, externalities of, 114, 121
food industry, dirty strategies of, 65, 71

Ford, 39, 43, 187
Ford Foundation, 187, 189
foreign direct investment (FDI) policies, 85
forest-dwelling communities, 13, 125–126
forestry and fishing, externalities of, 114, 121, 126
formal regulators, 83–87
for-profit businesses, 194, 196, 201, 209
fossil fuel industry, 114
  dirty strategies of, 63–64, 70
fossil fuel industry, externalities of, 114, 121, 126
Foxconn factory cities, 90
Foxconn India, 92
Foxconn model of manufacturing, 91, 93–94
fraud and data breaches, 116
free enterprise capitalism, 157–158, 166
free riding, contagion of, 163–168
Friedman, Milton, x
Frito Lay chips, 198

Gandhi, Mahatma, x
gatekeepers, 70
Gates, Bill and Melinda, 187
Gates Foundation, 187
General Electric, 192
General Motors, 39, 43
Generation One, ix
genetically modified foods, 117
GitHub, 164
Glaxo, 189
Global Climate Coalition (GCC), 64, 118
Google, 26, 65, 69–70, 103, 110, 195
  Android mobile operating system, 25
Gorilla Glass, 96–97
government sector, externalities of, 116, 123
greenhouse gases, 118
Grok chatbot, 139
grounded leadership, 120
5G technology, 117
Guan Yi, Dr, 3
The Guardian, 182, 185
guild system, 157
Gupta, Arvind, 82

Haidt, Jonathan, 118
Haier, 41
halo bias, 14
Hamburg, 158
Hart, Oliver, 137
Hassabis, Demis, 197–198
hate speech, 118
healthcare sector, externalities of, 116, 123
health literacy, 128
Hershey Company, 182, 184
Himalayan mindset, 58
Himalayan Mountain Challenge programme, 54–58
Hitler, Adolf, 198
hockey stick growth, 156–157
Holonyak Jr., Nick, 193

homophily, 14
Honda, 41
horn bias, 14
House of Cards (TV series), 104
Huawei, 41
Hughes Aircraft, 193
Human Rights Watch, 126
Hyundai, 41

IBM, 26–28, 191–192, 195
ICICI-Videocon case, 82
ICT revolution, 197
IKEA, 182, 187
illegal sand mining, 113–114
immersive listening, 13
Indian Council of Medical Research (ICMR), 95
The Indian Express, 82
Indian Institute of Science (IISc), Bangalore, 40, 184
Indian media industry, 86
Indian Migrant Crisis, 2020, 202
Indian Tobacco Company (ITC), 172, 199
  FMCG brands, 199
  supply chain capabilities, 198–199
India's economy, 41
Indigo
  capabilities, 28
  operational efficiency, 26–27
Industrial Revolution, 154
industrial towns in India, 43
  Bhilai, Chhattisgarh, 43
  Bokaro, Jharkhand, 43
  Durgapur, West Bengal, 43
  Jamshedpur (Tatanagar), 37, 41
  Kalinganagar, Odisha, 43
  Mithapur township, Gujarat, 40
  Rourkela, Odisha, 43
infant mortality, 154
inimitable business capabilities, 28, 33
innovation, 67, 90, 119
  clusters, 197
  ecosystem, 191–196
  locus of, 94–97
  transactional process, 93
integrated circuits (ICs), 192–193
Intel, 26, 192, 194
International Consortium of Investigative Journalists (ICIJ), 82
International Labour Organization (ILO), 38
Internet companies, dirty strategies of, 64–65, 71
investors, 99–100, 183
iodised salt, 200
issues, identifying, 17–18, 21
'I want it all' strategy, 28

Japanese manufacturing industries, 44, 90–91
Jenner Institute, 95
Jet Airways, 28
J.N. Tata Endowment, 182
Jobs, Steve, 33, 52–53, 97, 205

John Lewis Partnership, 172, 178
joint stock companies, 159
Jumper, John, 195–198
just world hypothesis, 14

Kaizen (continuous improvement), 30, 90
Kao, Charles K., 192, 195
keiretsu, 173, 177
Kia, 41
Kilby, Jack, 192
Kingfisher, 28
Korean chaebols, 173
Kyoto Protocol, 1997, 64

labelling and regulatory process, 146–148
labour costs, 44
labour-friendly policies, 37
labour movements, 36, 38–39, 47
labour unions, 44, 81
labour welfare studies, 39
land degradation, 113–114
layoffs, 100–102
'lead by example,' 50
leadership, 58, 208–209
  charismatic and grounded, 51–52
  grounded, 120
  sense of fairness and trust, 102
  under uncertainty, 2–5, 51
Lean manufacturing, 90
learning, 2
Lenovo, 41
light-emitting diodes (LEDs), 193, 195
limited liability partnerships (LLP), 172, 174, 179
Li Wenliang, Dr, 3
lobbying, 63–65
  against international climate agreements and national climate policies, 64
  regulation of, 73–74
  revolving door policy, 63
  by tobacco companies, 65
London, 157–158
London School of Economics, 39
Lonza Group, 95
low-cost locations, 44
Lübeck, 158
Lucas, Robert, 161
Lyft, 77

Maggi noodles, 198
Mahindra, 200
Maiman, Theodore, 193
Manekshaw, Sam, 50
manufacturing in East Asian countries, 90
manufacturing sector, externalities of, 114, 121, 126–127
Marconi, Guglielmo, 192
Marconi Company, 192
marginalised groups, x
market stakeholders, 81
  buyers, 74–75, 78, 179
  competitors, 74, 76–77, 79

customers, 74, 78
employees, 75–76, 78, 179
new innovative entrants, 74, 77, 79
suppliers, 74–75, 78, 179
Marx, Karl, x
McKinsey, 116, 178
media sector, externalities of, 116–117, 123
medieval economy of Europe, 157–158
mergers and acquisitions (M&A), 85
Meta, 100, 110, 131
methane emissions, 113
Metta meditation, 12
Mi, 41
Microsoft, 26, 65, 69–70, 179, 195
Windows, 110
Microsoft outage, 2024, 116
Mihm, Stephen, 101
mining industry, externalities of, 113–114, 121, 125–126
mis- and disinformation, 118
Mitsubishi, 173
mobile operating systems, 25, 110
Moderna, 95
Mokyr, Joel, 162
monopoly rights, 67
moral drift, 134–136, 138
Morrison, Toni, 210
Morton Salt Company, 200
motivation building excercise, 56–58
music streaming, 105. *see also* Spotify
Musk, Elon, 110, 136, 139–141

naïve realism, 14
Nakamura, Shuji, 193
Narmada Bachao Andolan, 126
National Cancer Grid, 182
National Centre for Performing Arts (NCPA), 41
National Institute of Health (NIH) Vaccine Research Centre, 95
National Institute of Virology (NIV), 95
needs, identifying, 17–18, 21
negative externalities of businesses, 63, 73, 84, 100, 118, 129, 136–137, 180, 191, 209
Nescafe, 198
Nestle, 198
Netflix, 102, 105
development of recommendation algorithms, 103–104
licensing agreements, 104
on-demand streaming model, 105
streaming service, 103–104
Netscape Navigator, 69
new innovative entrants, 77, 79
News Broadcasters and Digital Standards Authority (NBDSA), 86
Nichia Corporation, 193

Night (Elie Wiesel), 8
Nike, 75, 78
comprehensive Code of Conduct for suppliers, 75
Nintendo, 41
Nissan, 41
Nobel-winning physics discoveries, 191–194
Nokia, 25, 41, 191
non-market regulators, 81–82, 88
non-market stakeholders, 81, 134–136, 138, 146, 179–180
non-profit organisations (NGOs), 81, 88, 171, 201–202
Novo Nordisk, 182, 185
Novo Nordisk Foundation, 187
Noyce, Robert, 192
Nvidia, 26

Ohno, Taiichi, 30
Ola, 77
online hate and harassment, 128
online scams, 127–128
OpenAI, 26, 76, 78, 140, 195
operating system industry, 25, 69
Operation Warp Speed, 96
Optum, 109
'others,' 11
Ottoman Empire, 198
outgroup bias, 14
outsourcing, 44
overfishing and its impact, 126
overtime, 92
Oxford vaccine, 96

Palm Treo, 25
Panasonic, 41
Pandora, 102–103
Parle G, 199
patents, 67
Patriot Act, US, 84
Pepsi, 198
Pfizer- BioNTech vaccine, 95
pharmaceutical industry, 71
pharmaceutical industry, evergreening policies of, 66–67
pharmaceutical industry, externalities of, 115, 122
philanthrocapitalism, 169–172, 181
philanthropy-owned organisations. *see* enterprise foundations
Philip Morris, 65
Pirate Bay, 102
Pittsburgh, 43
pollution, 63–65, 73, 81, 100, 113–118, 126–128, 144, 148, 209
poor and vulnerable families, 128
Porter's forces, 24
power supply networks, 85
Premji, Azim, 183
Press Trust of India, 86
primitive societies, 13
private limited company, 172–173
privatisation, 166
process innovation, 25
producer cooperatives, 178

producer-owned organisations, 172, 175, 178
product innovation, 25
The Progress Principle (Theresa Amabile and Steven Kramer), 57
proximate factors, 18–19
Prozac, 67
psychological safety, 18
public goods and commons, 160–163, 196
  examples, 161–163
  non-excludable nature, 163
  remarkable, 162
  tragedy of commons, 164–165
  under-provision of, 165
public goods dilemma, 163–164
public healthcare, 165
publicly listed company, 172, 174

Ranbaxy scandal, 115
real estate industry, misleading claims of, 65–66, 71
Regional Advantage (AnnaLee Saxenian), 51
regulators
  formal, 83–88
  non-market, 81–82, 88
  private industry associations, 86
  regulatory capture, 87–88
  social media as, 83
  telecom, 84
  whistleblowers, 82
relational contracts, 31–32, 46, 93
Reliance, 173, 188
Reliance Foundation, 187
remote communities, 128
renewable energy industry, 114
renewable energy industry, externalities of, 114
reputational damage, 102
'revolving door' policy, 63
Rihanna, 111
Rolex, 182, 186
Roots of Empathy, 12
Russian Revolution of 1917, 38

safety and conditions, 92
salesperson, 129
Samsung, 41
Saudi Aramco, 173
Schawlow, Arthur, 193
Schumpeter, Joseph, 102
scientific management, 130–131
scientific thinking, 129
Searle, John, 11
Securities and Exchange Board of India (SEBI), 83, 86
self concept, 13
self-regulation, 147–148
semiconductor industry, externalities of, 115, 122
9 September 2001 attacks, 84
Serum Institute of India (SII), 94, 201
shakeout stage, 25
shareholder-centric business models, 177–178

shareholderism
  pros and cons, 45–46
  vs stakeholderism, 46–47
shareholder value maximisation, 136–137
Shockley, William, 192
Silicon Valley, 44, 51–52
  agility and adaptability of, 52
  communication mode, 51–52
Six Sigma, 88
slums, 127
smartphone industry, 25–27
  disruption of, 26
  early stage, 25
  growth stage, 25
  impact of artificial intelligence (AI), 26
  mature stage, 25–26
SmithKline Beecham, 189
social media, 6–7, 101, 119, 141, 147
  content moderation, 110, 139, 148
  public stakeholder scrutiny in, 135
  as regulators, 83
  targets of hate and harassment, 128, 144
social products, 140
social stratification, 156
soft drinks industry, 24
Sony, 41
SpaceX, 140
Spotify, 74–75, 78, 102–105
  business model, 104
  contracting innovations, 104
  freemium model, 104
  licensing deals, 104
stage of an industry
  early, 25
  growth, 25
  mature, 25–26
stakeholderism, 141
  externalities and, 144–146
  pros and cons, 45–46
  Toyota/Tata model of, 93–94
  vs shareholderism, 43–48
stakeholders, 202–206
  archetype, 16
  customers as, 16
  engagement, 16–17
  investors as, 97–98
  listing, 15–16
  maps, 151
  market, 138, 146
  non-market, 134–136, 138, 146, 179–180
Standard Telecommunication Laboratories, 192
standard work week, 92
Starbucks, 47, 75, 199
start-ups, 68, 72, 94–95, 99, 179, 195
state-owned enterprises (SOE), 172–173, 175
status quo bias, 14
Steel Authority of India Limited, 173
stereotyping, 14
'Still I Rise' (Maya Angelou), 9
stock exchanges, 157
stories, 7–9

listening to, 8–9
strategic design thinking, 119–120
strategic design thinking process
actionable points, identifying, 19–20
in IT, 27
listing stakeholders, 15–16
needs, wants, desires, issues and asks, identifying, 17–18
proximate and ultimate factors, identifying, 18–19
stakeholder engagement, 16–17
strategy, definition, 23
Sucher, Sandra, 101
Sunfeast, 199
suppliers, 74–75, 78
supply chain management, 97
supply chains, 197–199
surveillance capitalism, 118
surveillance system, 25
Swift, Taylor, 74, 78
Symbian, 25

Taj Hotel, 42
Tata, Jamsetji, 35–37, 205
Tata, J.R.D., 36, 206
Tata, Ratan, 42
Tata, Ratanji Dadabhoy, 40
Tata Group, 34–35, 47, 62, 173, 181–182, 184, 188, 205
commitment to stakeholders, 38, 42
establishment of Jamshedpur (Tatanagar), 37, 40, 99
Mithapur township, Gujarat, 40
philosophy of management, 35–37
revenue, 182
Tata Chemicals, 42
Tata Electronics, 92
Tata Motors, 42
Tata Power, 42
Tata Steel, 39, 40
as valuable brand, 41–42
vision, 206
worker-friendly policies, 36–37, 39, 76, 99
Tata Institute of Fundamental Research (TIFR), 41
Tata Institute of Social Sciences (TISS), 41, 182
Tata Medical Centre, 182
Tata Memorial Hospital, 41, 182
Tata Sons, 182
Tata Trusts, 182, 187
taxi industry, 77
teams, 56–58
technology sector, externalities of, 122
tech streaming businesses. *see* Netflix; Spotify
telecom industry, externalities of, 115–116
temporary workers, 92
Ten-second Barrier, 54
Tesla, 140, 195
Texas Instruments, 192, 194

textile and apparel industry, 114
textile and apparel industry, externalities of, 114, 122, 127
Thomsen, Steen, 190
time-bound private monopolies, 85
tobacco industry, 74, 78
tourism industry, externalities of, 117, 124
Townes, Charles, 193
Toyota, 41, 47–48, 50, 58, 90, 93
Toyota Production System (TPS), 29–31, 34, 44, 90, 94
  pillars of 'Toyota Way,' 31
Toyota/Tata model of stakeholderism, 93–94
training and development, 92
transport industry, externalities of, 115, 122
true leadership, 58
trust and trustworthy behaviou, 32
Turing, Alan, 194
twenty-first century, x
twenty-first-century manufacturing, 93
Twitter (X), 103, 110
  challenges, 140
  daily active users, 139
  expenses, 136
  lessons from, 139–140
  market capitalisation of, 135–136
  revenue-sharing model, 139
  shareholders, 137
  valuation, 136, 139–140
  X Hiring, 139
  X Premium, 139

Uber, 77
UK
  rise of 'labour' parties in, 38
  women's rights movement, 38
ultimate factors, 18–19
uncertainty, understanding of, 2–5
'UniEVerse' strategy, 41
Unilever, 47, 75, 199
United Airlines, 83
university-led clusters, 194
urgent and important tasks, 19–20
US Environmental Protection Agency (EPA), 63
US Federal Trade Commission, 83
US Food and Drug Administration (FDA), 83, 86
US Lunar Mission, 1960s, 205
US opioid crisis, 116
US Tax Reform Act, 1969, 189
US tobacco industry, 65, 71

vaccine development during COVID-19 pandemic, 94–96
  side effects, 117
vacuum tube, 192
vision for new world, 205–206
Vistara, 28
vulnerable people, 127–128

Walmart, 27, 75, 85, 173
wants, identifying, 17–18, 21
waste management and recycling industry, externalities of, 117, 124
Wells, H.G., x
Westner, Marilyn Morgan, 101
whistleblowers, 82, 150
Wikipedia, 164
Windows Mobile, 25
winning, 57
Wipro, 182–183, 188
worker-centrism, 29
worker democracy, 181
worker-driven continuous improvement, 30
work–life balance, 92
World Wide Web, 195
World Wide Web Consortium (W3C), 195

Xavier Labour Relations Institute (XLRI), 41

Yahoo, 65
YouTube, 103

zero-defect system, 90
Zingales, Luigi, 137
Zuboff, Shoshana, 118
Zuckerberg, Mark, 131

Acknowledgements

This book is a result of interactions with many outstanding scholars over the years. I would like to thank Brian Richter (Texas), with whom I developed the idea of corporate stewardship which this book draws from; Raghuram Rajan (Chicago) and Luigi Zingales (Chicago), whose research helped me understand the basics of a more wholesome 'Chicago school' of economics; Joel Mokyr (Northwestern), Paola Sapienza (Northwestern) and Deirdre McCloskey (UIC), whose work and mentorship on culture and history of progress has created the foundation of all my work; Simcha Jong (UCL) and Sheilagh Ogilvie (Oxford), whose research introduced me to the relational world of clusters and guilds that formed the core ideas of my research; Trilochan Sastry (IIMB, Association for Democratic Reforms, Farm Veda) and Kiran Seth (IITD, SPIC MACAY), whose grounded actionable work at the grassroots of development has been a true inspiration; and Vikram Kohli (SPA Bhopal), with whom I developed the strategic design thinking process that forms the core philosophy of this book.

I owe much of my intellectual heritage to the Stigler Center for the Study of the Economy and the State at the University of Chicago and my long-term fellowship (since 2016) at the Center. I want to thank the Center for providing me with an academic background to pursue research on topics at the interface of business, economy and the state, directly relevant to this book.

I would also like to thank my colleagues in the Strategy area at IIM Bangalore, who helped me learn the basics of Strategy 101 while teaching the Competition and Strategy (C&S) course to nearly 450 students since 2018. I would finally like to acknowledge my nearly 350 students at IIMB since 2022 who took my Strategic Stewardship elective and have effectively co-created this book with me, as well as my wonderful colleagues Gaurav G.B, Sumedha Biswas and especially Janvhi Mishra, who helped me curate the course.

I cannot thank my editor, Aurodeep, enough, who has been such a delight to work with and helped me bring out the vision of this book so lucidly. I am grateful to my parents and sister, Priyanka, for their unabated support, the trustful friendship of Aditi, Anjul, Ashish, Manaswini, Nilam and Nitesh and the inspiring company of Jaspreet throughout this writing journey. This book would not be possible without the beautiful community that supported me.

Thank you!

'Supposing I have come by a fair amount of wealth—either by way of legacy or by means of trade and industry—I must know that all that wealth does not belong to me; what belongs to me is the right to an honourable livelihood, no better is the right to an honourable livelihood, no better than that enjoyed by millions of others. The rest of my wealth belongs to the community and must be used for the welfare of the community.' —Mahatma Gandhi